The Book of *Sports Lists #3*

It was hand-written and it came from a place called Pacific Palisades, California. "I hope this might be helpful," Ronald Reagan wrote two years ago when he selected his "6 Greatest Sports Movies" for *The Book of Sports Lists.*

Even Ronald Reagan makes lists, and, as it happened, his list was the opener. And, appropriately, President Reagan leads off #3.

Unlike hula hoops and mini-skirts, list-making is not a passing fad. The response from readers and contributors assures that this is an on-going game that any number can play.

We thank those who responded to our request for lists, and we express regrets to those whose lists did not make #3. But there is always #4.

We invite you to participate. Send your list to:

Associated Features
370 Lexington Avenue
New York, NY 10017

Remember, not everyone can get to be president. But you might make *The Book of Sports Lists.*

Also by Phil Pepe and Zander Hollander:

The Book of Sports Lists
The Book of Sports Lists #2

BY PHIL PEPE AND
ZANDER HOLLANDER

An Associated Features Book

PINNACLE BOOKS NEW YORK

Dedicated to:

1. **400,000 purchasers of *The Book of Sports Lists #1 and #2***
2. **319 creative friends who contributed.**

EDITORS' NOTE: This list is not necessarily in order of preference.

THE BOOK OF SPORTS LISTS #3

An original Pinnacle Books edition, published for the first time anywhere.

First printing, August 1981

ISBN: 0-523-41444-7

Cover photos by Focus on Sports

Printed in the United States of America

PINNACLE BOOKS, INC.
1430 Broadway
New York, New York 10018

Contents

III BATTER UP

I

On The Air

Ronald Reagan and 4 Other Sports Broadcasters Who Went On to Bigger Things

1. Ronald Reagan—The President, who played right guard for Eureka College in Illinois, successfully auditioned for a sports announcing job at WOC in Davenport, Iowa, after his graduation in 1931. He broadcast University of Iowa games and later moved up to WHO in Des Moines. He covered the Chicago Cubs in spring training in 1936 and subsequently did re-creations of Cubs games off the Western Union wire.

   While in Los Angeles, he took the screen test that led to an acting career that included two sports movies (*Knute Rockne—All-American,* in which he played George Gipp, and *The Winning Team,* in which he was pitcher Grover Cleveland Alexander). The rest is history.
2. Walter Cronkite—Before he became a distinguished journalist at UPI and a world figure as a TV commentator at CBS, Walter Cronkite was a sports broad-

Ronald Reagan as a sports announcer in the mid-1930s at WHO in Des Moines, Iowa.

Wide World

After his sportscasting days, Paul Douglas played a variety of roles, including this one (center) in "The Guy Who Came Back."
Sports Photo Source

caster for a small local station while still a student at the University of Texas.

3. Jay C. Flippen—A comedian and character actor whose career spanned more than half a century, "Colonel Jay C. Flippen" broadcast New York Yankee baseball games in the early 1930s.
4. Paul Douglas—He was best known for his Broadway role as a rugged junk tycoon in *Born Yesterday*, but in the early 1930s, Paul Douglas was a well-known sports announcer. It was from sports that he branched into assignments as announcer-straight-man for comedians Jack Benny, Fred Allen, George Burns and Gracie Allen. And then he starred in many films.

5. Ford Frick—On the way to becoming Commissioner of Baseball, Ford Frick was a newspaperman, Babe Ruth's ghost writer, and a noted sports announcer. He and Stan Lomax, then fellow writers on the New York *Journal,* broke into radio as a team in 1930. Lomax, in an interview several decades later, told broadcaster-historian Ted Patterson, "Ford could re-create a ball game on radio better than any man I have ever heard, and I have listened to them all over the years.

   "I'll never forget a game we were re-creating when the New York Giants were in Chicago to play the Cubs. During the course of the game, there was a fire outside Wrigley Field and the wires leading to the relay station caught fire. We were cut off from what was happening on the field. Ford had a batter fouling off the pitch about eight times. Then he followed with a lengthy argument between the umpires and the two managers. For 10 minutes he filled in with pure cleverness and imagination. He was an amazing person."

Edwin Pope's 7 Best Sports-Oriented TV Commercials

A little old listmaker from way back, Edwin Pope is sports editor and columnist for the Miami *Herald.* Others of his lists are sprinkled throughout these pages.

1. Joe Greene for soda pop
2. Pete Rose for after-shave
3. Nick Buoniconti-Norm Crosby for beer
4. Bubba Smith for beer
5. Muhammad Ali for roach killer
6. Boog Powell for beer
7. Joe Namath for popcorn popper

Stan Isaacs' 10 Jocks Whose TV Sales Spiels Are Eminently Resistible

As TV sports critic for Long Island's *Newsday,* Stan Isaacs must endure more commercials than most of us.

Pete Rose hustles on and off the base-paths.

Aqua Velva/Sports Photo Source

1. Joe Namath
2. Bruce Jenner
3. Mark Spitz
4. Wilt Chamberlain
5. Phil Rizzuto
6. Arnold Palmer
7. Joe (Why Have You Come Back This Way?) DiMaggio
8. Don Meredith
9. Muhammad Ali
10. Peggy Fleming

Stan Isaacs' 10 New Merchandising Concepts That Could Spin Off from the Sasson Boxing Trunks Worn Recently by Matthew Saad Muhammad

1. Gucci sweatsocks
2. Tiffany tennis balls
3. Buster Brown hockey skates
4. Christian Dior hockey sticks
5. Yves St. Laurent boxing gloves
6. AMF bras
7. Hillerich & Bradsby pickles
8. Dr. Denton shoulder pads
9. Mark Fore & Strike baseball gloves
10. Helena Rubinstein bats

8 Sports Personalities Who Switched

A few years ago, the Miller Brewing Co. received kudos, and increased sales, for its clever commercials depicting former athletes. As a retaliatory campaign, competitor Anheuser-Busch wooed several of Miller's former jocks over to its product, Natural Light Beer, with the pronouncement that these men switched. "Taste is why you'll switch," is the company slogan. Taste, that is, in nice clothes, big cars, and large bank accounts.

1. Mickey Mantle
2. Walt Frazier
3. Joe Frazier
4. Sonny Jurgensen
5. Gordie Howe
6. Catfish Hunter
7. Tom Lasorda
8. Nick Buoniconti

The Natural Light all-stars include, standing from left, Mickey Mantle, Walt Frazier, Joe Frazier, "Captain" Norm Crosby, and Gordie Howe. Up front are Sonny Jurgensen and Catfish Hunter. Tommy Lasorda and Nick Buoniconti are regulars, but they missed the photo.

Anheuser-Busch/Sports Photo Source

Willie Schatz's New York *Daily News* Ratings of 8 Pro Football Play-by-Play Announcers and 11 Pro Football TV Analysts

Note: Ratings are on a scale of 1 to 10 with 1 being agony and 10 being ecstasy. Five is flunking.

PLAY-BY-PLAY

1. Dick Enberg, 9.5—Gives you what you need to know when you need to know it without intruding on the game. Not afraid to take a back seat and defer to the analyst, which is as it should be. Would that his colleagues would learn such manners. Consistently manages to be informative and helpful without being obnoxious, but has developed tendency to wax overly

Dick Enberg, left, and Merlin Olsen top the ratings.

NBC-TV/Sports Photo Source

poetic. If he swallows a tranquilizer now and then, he can be a 10.

2. Frank Gifford, 8.5—The Giffer's come a long way. Smooth, pleasant delivery, although still can be too excitable. Has become more announcer and less jock in the last few years. Informative, concise, and not overbearing about former life and times as superstar. Has done his homework and become a polished professional. Scores sympathy points for tolerating Monday Night Madness. Now if he'd just be more critical of sins on the field. Can be a 9 if he tells it like it is more often.
3. Vince Scully, 7.5—Suffers by comparison with his baseball work, where he's the main man. Knowledgeable and informative, but goes overboard on statistics and tends to intrude on the game too much. Needs to remember that, unlike baseball, football requires little talking. Gets too excited at wrong times. But still gives the basics as well as anyone. Capable of rising to challenge of big event.
4. Charley Jones, 7—Gives the facts with no fuss, no muss. Knows his place and rarely intrudes. Down-home, folksy style adds interesting flavor to 42-0 romp in its fourth quarter. But can be too matter-of-fact on one play, then make the next sound like Armageddon. Too lax on players' and officials' mistakes. Reluctant to criticize either on the air. Has good potential to move up a point.
5. Don Criqui, 7—Good mix of humor and irreverence. Far cry from previous life as cheerleader/apologist. Not afraid to criticize either officials or players. Not that good at giving basics. Gets too excited too quickly and makes presence felt too frequently. Needs to clean and polish act before becoming serious contender.
6. Gary Bender, 6—Doesn't turn you on or off. Basically does his job and doesn't bother viewers. Informative and knowledgeable, but doesn't seem to have energy and vitality of those ranked higher. Needs more electricity if plans to light future fires.
7. Curt Gowdy, 4—A nice guy who tries hard. But he hasn't been able to recapture smoothness and professionalism of his earlier days. Talks too much, too often.

Frequently gives unnecessary information. Hasn't learned to let action do the talking. When he relaxes and does his homework, can still be enjoyable.

8. Pat Summerall, 3—Formerly among best, now tries to be cute, inside, and macho and fails at all three. Too much ex-jock and not enough announcer. Consistent practitioner of protectionist philosophy. Too many jokes at expense of facts. Has lost ability to keep viewers interested. Better for sleeping than Sominex.

Analysts

1. Merlin Olsen, 9.5—Even if you didn't care about something before he explains it, you will when he finishes. Calm, perceptive, lucid technique makes you wish he'd been your only college professor for four years. Works long, hard hours and watches more film than a movie critic to stay current, which helps him give you a replay before you see it.
2. John Madden, 9—Former Oakland Raider coach lends knowledge, humor, and insight and comes out with enjoyable, informative style. Keeps events and games in perspective. Leaves listeners wanting more. Not afraid to criticize players, coaches, officials, or himself. Enthusiasm is refreshing but not intrusive. Still makes mistakes, but experience should rectify that. Not worried about getting coaching job back, as are a few colleagues.
3. Bob Trumpy, 9—Former Cincinnati Bengal tight end is almost all announcer. Earned points in 1980 for pointing out differences in Raider tackle Art Shell's stance on running and passing plays, then consistently predicting play. Knows game well and can share knowledge without being condescending. Insightful and calm.
4. Len Dawson, 7—Vastly improved from quarterbacking days in Kansas City when he couldn't say anything longer than a cadence count. Pleasant, informative style. Has begun to criticize more and protect less. Needs to become more sure of himself and share more

of his inside knowledge. More aggressiveness and confidence will move him to next echelon.

5. Don Meredith, 7—Has gotten more comfortable and secure in role, to his and listeners' benefit. No longer tries to be comedian so frequently, although still has tendency to force humor when it isn't there. Still as likable as ever. Acting more like skilled analyst and less like fun-loving ex-quarterback. The more of that behavior, the better. Has to continue the journey, but is getting closer to the promised mike.
6. John Brodie, 6—Another ex-quarterback (San Francisco) who has begun to blossom. Slowly discarding perfectionist shell he wore for so long. Now less afraid to criticize one of his own for bad play or call. Good at explaining philosophy of particular play or series without too many technicalities, though talks too much. Manages to keep game in perspective, knowing that tomorrow will be here as usual.
7. Hank Stram, 6—The best predictor this side of Jeane Dixon. Even an ex-coach shouldn't be so successful at calling plays. Of course, had he been this good at New Orleans or Kansas City, he'd still be coaching. And he'd obviously like to be again, as he makes clear in most comments. Needs to stop looking for another job and pay more attention to this one.
8. Howard Cosell, 4—This hurts because he is still the most fearless of the breed. A lousy play is a lousy play. But it takes 50 words or more to realize it and 40 of them are banalities and trivialities. Reached peak of pomposity, arrogance, conceit, and condescension in 1980. "Exactly right, Frank (or Danderoo)." "As I was saying . . ." How about as someone else was saying?
9. Tom Brookshier, 3—Descending as rapidly as partner Summerall. Knows game well, but hides ability and insight behind smarmy locker room veneer. Hasn't been a cornerback for a long time, but he still must miss it because he's really into violence and hitting. Car makers should protect their own as well as he does. No bad plays, although he will acknowledge bad calls.
10. Fran Tarkenton, 2—One of (ABC Sports President)

Roone Arledge's rare errors. Every play is a great one. Every series is Armageddon. Obviously hasn't been away from it long enough to be realistic. Has tried to tone down from rookie year, but how could he not do so? "That's incredible" may be, but Tark isn't.

11. George Allen, 1—After three years of unemployment, still a coach first, last, and always. Lets us in on how he would have done everything, which of course is different than how the coach on the field is doing it. Favorite word is "I," closely followed by "we." Occasionally can admit that Dallas Cowboys know what they're doing and Tom Landry is not too bad a coach. Once in a while tells you something you didn't know.

II

Arts and Letters

Dewey Selmon's 6 Favorite Philosophers

Note: Dewey Selmon, linebacker for the Tampa Bay Buccaneers, is a candidate for a Ph.D. in philosophy.

1. Plato—"I'm most comfortable with Plato's world of ideas. Even though it's not a world that can be felt or touched, it's there."
2. Augustine—"A very honest man constantly tempted by the sensual world. He would acknowledge doing wrong, say he would do better and then do wrong again. He reminds me of some of our current politicians."
3. Bonaventure—"Bonaventure was one of the big three—with Augustine and Aristotle—to bring back theology."
4. Socrates—"He raises a lot of questions against the concepts of Plato. Even though I am most comfortable with Plato, I admire a good challenge."
5. Spinoza—"A true realist."
6. Aristotle—"First challenge to Socrates and Plato."

SOURCE: *Inside Sports*

Plato never played football, but he's Dewey Selmon's quarterback.

UPI

Dewey Selmon prepped for philosophy and the pros at Oklahoma.
Oklahoma/Sports Photo Source

Herman Masin's 18 Pieces of Graffiti That Stand the Best Chance of Making the Outside Wall of Any Hall of Fame

Herman Masin, who always puns on fourth down, is editor of *Scholastic Coach* magazine.

1. Anyone who beats Army is rotten to the corps.
2. If Lloyd Free and Ray Williams opened a pawnshop, they'd have to hang six balls out in front.
3. Joe Pepitone is now using AstroTurf on his head. ("You get a better bounce and it cuts down on the maintenance.")
4. If Lauren Bacall married Al Oerter, couldn't she run on the Lauren Oerter ticket?
5. Always trust a pitcher over 30 victories.
6. Duane Bobick is an artist who believes in getting as close to the canvas as possible when he works.
7. Gaylord Perry's 3.67 ERA was more than he expectorated.
8. Pete Rozelle built the world in six days. On the seventh, he sold the rights to ABC.
9. Pete Rose likes the daily double.
10. Flattery will get you no hair with Howard Cosell.
11. The Boston Bruins aren't very funny, but they keep you in stitches.
12. Does Jimmy the Greek know what's bets for him?
13. If Kurt Thomas vaults over Reggie Jackson, will they name a parallel bar after him?
14. If the Titanic hit Tom Landry, wouldn't it sink?
15. If peace is declared in the Near East, will Bob Hope spend next Christmas visiting hospitals in the Philadelphia Phillies' locker room?
16. If Fran Tarkenton keeps knocking his old pro coach, won't he wind up in Bud Grant's tomb?
17. Don't raise the baskets in basketball, lower the floors.
18. True Grit is Willie Aikens fielding a ground ball.

Harvey Sabinson's "10 Broadway Musicals and Plays with Particular Appeal for My Friend, Red Holzman, Coach of the New York Knicks"

Harvey Sabinson is a self-described penetrating guard for the League of New York Theatres and Producers, and an inveterate Knicks fan.

1. "The Elephant Man"—Red drafts a center eight feet tall and six feet wide, and devises the elephant defense in which everybody stands around eating peanuts and dropping the shells on the court.
2. "Peter Pan"—Red finally finds that small forward he's been seeking. The guy's feet never touch the floor since he's suspended from the Garden ceiling by wires.
3. "Mornings at Seven"—As a disciplinary measure, Red institutes practice sessions at 7 A.M. The first one to be fined for lateness is Red himself, when his Long Island Railroad train from Cedarhurst is delayed.
4. "The Play's the Thing"—Red finally finds the answer to schoolyard basketball.
5. "Philadelphia, Here I Come"—Red takes his team to the Spectrum in a jubilant mood when he finds that four 76ers starters are on the disabled list.
6. "The Four Poster"—Red puts four big centers in the middle to clog up the keyhole.
7. "Jumpers"—Red finds five starters who can get offensive rebounds.
8. "Traveling Lady"—The Knicks sign a woman star from Old Dominion. Red releases her when she's called for street walking.
9. "Billion Dollar Baby"—Red gets his dream center when the Knicks sign a 14-year-old junior high school star to a multi-year, billion-dollar contract.
10. "The Happy Time"—The Knicks win the playoffs again.

Irving Rudd's 14 Songs About Sports That Never Made the Hit Parade

1. "Life's a Game of Polo"
2. "Joltin' Joe DiMaggio"
3. "Benny, the Bow-Legged Bowler"
4. "Say Hey, Willie Mays"
5. "I Love Mickey (Mantle)"
6. "I Fell Asleep at the Football Game"
7. "I Met Her at the Grey Cup"
8. "Leave Us Go Root for the Dodgers, Rodgers"
9. "Hey Sugar Ray (Leonard)"
10. "Since They're All Playing Miniature Golf"
11. "Son of a Halfback"
12. "When She and I Go Skiing By"
13. "Goodnight, Little Leaguer, Goodnight"
14. "With All the Bases Loaded, I Struck Out"

Edwin Pope's 10 Worst Interviews

1. Thurman Munson
2. Duane Thomas
3. Tom Weiskopf
4. Lawrence McCutcheon
5. Ben Hogan
6. Pancho Gonzales
7. Darrell Johnson
8. Ilie Nastase
9. Oscar Bonavena
10. Mark Spitz

Bill Libby's 15 Most Interesting Interviews

Bill Libby has been interviewing sports personalities for newspaper and magazine articles, and for more than 60 books, over the last 30 years. In a previous *Book of Sports Lists,* he listed 15 "good guys" and 15 "bad guys" as far as willingness to talk to the media, not as good or bad interviews. Here he lists not the most accessible subjects, who are always willing to talk but do not have much to say, nor the most flamboyant, who talk only about themselves with a sort of tunnel vision, but those stars—and it is limited to stars—who seemed to him the most interesting.

Bill Russell in his last coaching job at Seattle. *George Gojkovich*

1. Bill Russell—If you can get to him, you will get a lot out of him. He looks at his game of basketball, and at life, in a different way from most of us and he was one of the few who made me look at life in a new way.
2. Reggie Jackson—Ego be damned, he is an absolutely honest man who sees beneath the surface of things and made me see what the life of a superstar really is like.
3. Gordie Howe—A man of little formal education, but of an innate intelligence, who uses a marvelous sense of humor to see things as they are.
4. Maury Wills—Another athlete who always saw beneath the surface of things. His skin, however, may have thinned since he became a manager.
5. Stirling Moss—A man who was able to make you feel what it was like to take part in a sport—car racing—most of us would fear.
6. El Cordobes—Another man who could make you feel the thrill of a dangerous sport—bullfighting—despite having to use a translator.
7. Merlin Olsen—An intellectual who could cut to the heart of life in his complicated sport, professional football.
8. Ken Dryden—Another intellectual who taught you something about a sport you thought you knew—hockey.
9. Rod Hundley—Subject of the best book I ever did because he was willing to talk with great good humor about being one of those athletes who plays hardest off the court.
10. John Carlos—The great "black glove" Olympic runner who made me understand better than any other product of a black ghetto what it was like.
11. Billie Jean King—Outspoken and revealing about what it is like to be a woman athlete.
12. Chi Cheng—Maybe I have not interviewed as many women athletes as I would have liked, but this spectacular sprinter made me see what it was like to be both a woman and an athlete.
13. Kareem Abdul-Jabbar—When you can get to him, he is

one of those who looks at life differently than most do and is fascinating.

14. Bill Walton—When I got to him, he made me feel what a young athlete concerned with today's troubled world was feeling.
15. Tony Lema—Another free-spirit who articulated well what it is like to like the good life as well as the athletic life.

Libby adds: "Some other fascinating fellows I have met include managers and coaches Al McGuire, John McKay, Frank Leahy, George Allen, Don Cherry, Fred Shero, Wren Blair, Casey Stengel, Joe Lapchick, Lou Holtz, Pete Newell, and Bill Sharman; and broadcasters Vince Scully, Red Barber, Marty Glickman, Dick Enberg, Chick Hearn, and Ted Husing."

Frank Boggs' Top 10 Seasons

Frank Boggs is sports editor of the Colorado Springs *Sun* and, obviously, a man for all seasons.

1. Autumn
2. Baseball
3. Spring
4. Pro football
5. Golf
6. Summer
7. College football
8. Opera
9. (tie) Winter and ice hockey

Pete Enich's 11 Football Parables in the Bible

"It all started on November 6, 1869, in a park in New Brunswick, N.J., where a group of Princeton students and another group from Rutgers, 25 to a side, met in the first formal game of intercollegiate football," writes Pete Enich, Kansas City (Kans.) public safety information officer and sports trivia expert.

"Did I say formal? The formality went only so far as it was a scheduled event, a challenge issued and a challenge accepted.

What it was was hardly football as we now know it, a germ of an infection that would sweep the nation, a sport unique anywhere in the world, 'The Great American Autumnal Madness.'

"But uniquely American? This absurdity has been forcefed to us for more than a century. Blocking, tackling and running with an inflated bladder irrefutably dates back to another era. By searching the scriptures of the Bible, we find many texts suited to the gridiron and how the game of football should be played."

1. "Speak that they go forward." Exodus, 14.15—Signals appeared in 1883, originally masked in casual phrases or a single word, but Walter Camp and his cronies were thousands of years tardy in this area.
2. "Require a sign." 1 Corinthians, 1:22—Evidence of Biblical quarterbacks.
3. "Hold up my goings in thy paths, that my footsteps slip not." Psalms, 17:5—Warriors in the Old Testament were no different than today's opponents. They sought the winning edge in a crucial game. This prayer of David also hints that many of the stadiums in Biblical lore were without artificial turf.
4. "Mine enemies reproach me all day and they that are mad against me are sworn against me." Psalms, 102.8—The post-game lament first appeared in the Old Testament and has been echoed through the years. Many coaches find it quite appropriate today.
5. "They rush with one accord." Acts, 19:29—Jimmy Brown, O.J. Simpson, Earl Campbell, Tony Dorsett . . . prolific ground-gainers all. The Bible disclosed some solid ball-carriers, too.
6. "Many shall run to and fro." Daniel, 12.4—Indicates a polished wishbone offense contrary to Darrell Royal's pride of authorship in the late 1960s.
7. "Trample them." Isaiah, 63:3—The 1884 season introduced a milestone in football, soon to be a controversial one. Against Penn, Princeton turned up with the "V" trick, forerunner of the flying wedge. Ten men formed a close V-shaped mass with the ball-carrier at the apex, forward. Once in motion, the mass was difficult to

break through. It was thought to be the first step toward putting interference ahead of the runner, which was illegal at the time. Actually, Isaiah outlined the wedge quite succinctly.

8. "Run not to excess." 1 Peter, chapter 4, verse 4—The first reported pep talk by a mentor, obviously the plea of a disgruntled defensive line coach.
9. "Time to kill." Ecclesiastes, 3:3—Fielding H. (Hurry Up) Yost became head coach at Michigan in 1901 and built his famed "point-a-minute" teams which labeled the Wolverines as the most powerful dynasty the game had witnessed. In five seasons, 1901-1905, Michigan rolled up 2,821 points to 42 for the opposition. Logically, the Wolverines always had plenty of time to kill after the first 30 minutes.
10. "Therefore will I scatter them as the stubble that passeth away by the wind of the wilderness." Jeremiah, 13:24—All the ingredients for an excellent middle linebacker, obviously skeptical of his teammates' ability.
11. "The tacklings are loose." Isaiah, 33:23—The first recorded apology behind a defeat, the kind for which football coaches have since become noted.

Jerome Holtzman's 30 Best Baseball Books

Author and anthologist, Jerome Holtzman is a veteran sportswriter for the Chicago *Sun-Times.*

1. *The Suitors of Spring,* by Pat Jordan
2. *The Long Season,* by Jim Brosnan
3. *Veeck, as in Wreck,* by Bill Veeck with Ed Linn
4. *Ball Four,* by Jim Bouton and Leonard Shecter
5. *Now Wait a Minute, Casey,* by Maury Allen
6. *The Glory of Their Times,* by Lawrence Ritter
7. *My Life in Baseball: The True Record,* by Ty Cobb with Al Stump
8. *The Boys of Summer,* by Roger Kahn
9. *The Natural,* by Bernard Malamud
10. *The Great American Novel,* by Philip Roth
11. *The Summer Game,* by Roger Angell

12. *You Know Me, Al,* by Ring Lardner
13. *Baseball,* by Dr. Harold Seymour
14. *100 Years of Baseball,* by Lee Allen
15. *The Thinking Man's Guide to Baseball,* by Leonard Koppett
16. *Baseball Is a Funny Game,* by Joe Garagiola
17. *Baseball's Greatest Teams,* by Tom Meany
18. *The Kid From Tompkinsville,* by John Tunis
19. *The Days of Mr. McGraw,* by Joe Durso
20. *The Year the Yankees Lost the Pennant,* by Douglas Wallop
21. *Yaz,* by Carl Yastrzemski and Al Hirshberg
22. *The Universal Baseball Assn., Inc.,* by Robert Coover
23. *The Quality of Courage,* by Mickey Mantle and Robert Creamer
24. *Babe,* by Robert Creamer
25. *McGraw of the Giants,* by Frank Graham
26. *Jackie Robinson, My Own Story,* by Jackie Robinson and Wendell Smith
27. *Baseball,* by Robert Smith
28. *The Only Game in Town,* by Charles Einstein
29. *The Making of a Manager,* by Russ Schneider
30. *The Ten Thousand Dollar Arm,* by Charles Van Loan

Says Holtzman: "This list is in no order of preference. I tried to limit my list to 10, but found it would be difficult, also unfair."

Editor's Note: No list of Best Sports Books would be complete without Jerome Holtzman's *No Cheering in the Press Box.*

18 NHL Players' Favorite Books

1. Lee Fogolin—*Sports in North America*
2. Richard Martin—*National Geographic*
3. Robbie Ftorek—*Uncle Remus Stories of Brer Bear, Brer Rabbit, Brer Fox*
4. Gordie Roberts—*Rich Man, Poor Man*
5. Al McAdam—*Lord of the Rings*

6. Wayne Babych—*The Bible*
7. Bengt-Ake Gustaffson—*Papillon*
8. Guy Charron—*QB VII*
9. Jim Bedard—*The Exorcist*
10. Dennis Maruk—*The Exorcist*
11. Garry Unger—*Animal Farm*
12. Ron Grahame—*Complete Book of Short Stories of Sherlock Holmes*
13. Charlie Simmer—*Salem's Lot*
14. Ted Bulley—*The Manitou*
15. Paul Reinhart—*Shogun*
16. Robert Picard—*Maison Des Damnes*
17. Ryan Walters—*Centennial*
18. Brian Engblom—*Marathon Man*

SOURCE: *Goal* Magazine

Herb Kamm's Terrific Typewriter Team: The Greatest Baseball Writers and Cartoonist in New York in the '40s, '50s, and '60s

A former sportswriter for the Asbury Park (N.J.) *Press,* Herb Kamm is editor of the Cleveland *Press.*

1b Dan Daniel, *World-Telegram* (even though he never hit a home run out of Yankee Stadium)
2b Milt Gross, *Post*
3b W. C. Heinz, *Sun*
ss John Drebinger, *Times*
lf Jimmy Powers, *News*
cf Bill Corum, *Journal-American*
rf Dan Parker, *Mirror*
c Joe Williams, *World-Telegram*
dh Willard Mullin, *World-Telegram*
p Stanley Woodward, *Herald Tribune*
p Jimmy Cannon, *Journal-American*

Says Kamm: "They had power, they had speed, they had class. They were to sportswriting what the '27 Yankees were to baseball, and they were no slouches at the watering holes, either."

Note: While Red Smith, *Times,* and Dick Young, *News,* were heavy hitters in the decades of the '40s, '50s and '60s, Herb Kamm eliminated them from consideration for his team because they are still active and part of the "modern" era. The designated cartoonist, of course, is Willard Mullin.

Dave Camerer's 5 Special Sporting Recollections

Dave Camerer, newspaperman, magazine sports editor, radio writer, author or coauthor of nine books, including one of sport's all-time best-sellers, Grantland Rice's *The Tumult and the Shouting,* majored in English at Dartmouth and minored, he says, in football under Earl (Red) Blaik. He was on the line in 1935 on the day of Dartmouth's twelfth-man classic at Princeton. As a sports writer on the New York *World-Telegram* before World War II, Dave got to cover the Brooklyn Dodgers, among other assignments that he fulfilled with a youthful enthusiasm that is his trademark to this day.

1. Dartmouth's 12th Man, November 23, 1935—Legend insists he was an inebriated clown in a raccoon coat and derby. Stiff he may have been, but he wore only a grey moleskin windbreaker, blond crew-cut, and a Barbara Fritchie stare.

   It was a snowy day and there was a sellout crowd of 56,000 at Princeton's Palmer Stadium to see two undefeated Ivies. Princeton led, 13-6, at the half and then made it 19-6 in the third quarter. Now it was late in the fourth, with the ball on our six, but we held them to only three yards on two rushes. On third down, as left guard Joe Handrahan and I lined up, out of that swirling blizzard there emerged an incredible sight. A spectator had splashed across the end zone onto the playing field and he stumbled into place on the line between Handrahan and me. He shouted, "Kill them

Princeton bums!'' and he flung himself into the Tiger backfield where, face down, he passed out. In the ensuing snarl the ball advanced to our one, where, inexplicably, the officials let it be. The whole Princeton line manhandled the poor guy unmercifully until the state troopers collared him and dragged him off, his heels cutting a double track in the snow.

P.S. Princeton scored on the next play. Final score: 26-6.

2. Second Joe Louis-Max Schmeling fight, at Yankee Stadium, June 22, 1938—I was seated with my best girl in the overflow press section behind second base as the bell sounded for Round 1. During the time it took a Cafe Society pair to rummage by us and past a small, bespectacled gent on my right, the fight was past tense, Louis a knockout winner at 2:04 of the first round.

   ''Goddammit,'' screamed the little guy next to me. ''I fly all the way from the coast to see this fight and I don't see one (bleeping) punch.''

3. Night Train, July 1938—The Dodgers had split a Sunday doubleheader in St. Louis, winning the nightcap on a homer by Brooklyn outfielder Ernie Koy. Standing small beside the huge coal-burning, multi-stack freight engine in the St. Louis yards were our several cars, press included, that had been coupled behind a string of baggage cars, destination Chicago. It was near midnight, hot and sultry, and I chatted with the engineer, friendly if imperious in his high cab. I wore slacks and a short-sleeved sport shirt.

   ''Ain't you Ernie Koy?'' he said.

   ''Yup.''

   ''I saw you hit that homer. What kinda pitch was it?''

   ''Fast ball . . . cock high.'' Then: ''Where's your coal shoveler?''

   ''Don't need none. Not with this baby. Automatic feeder.''

Inevitably, I had to ask the $64 question. Might I ride up there with him to the first stop?

''Sorry Ernie . . . against the rules of the road.''

Dave Camerer, who figured in Dartmouth's twelfth-man oddity and the Grantland Rice autobiography, celebrates publication of *The Tumult and The Shouting* with some of Granny's gang at Toots Shor's in 1954. It would have been Granny's 74th birthday. Left to right: Yogi Berra, Lou Little, Camerer, Toots, and Eddie Arcaro.

Bill Mark/Sports Photo Source

Moments later the conductor waved his all-aboard lantern.

"Better get back to your car," the engineer drawled. "We're about to haul ass."

"How far to the next stop?"

"Near 150 miles. Water stop."

"I'll get off there. They'll never know."

He studied me. Ernie Koy's hair was straight and Indian black . . . mine, crew-cut and ginger. Then, looking both ways, he pointed to the foothold and beckoned me aboard.

Since that night 40-some years ago I've ridden considerable conveyances to a considerable number of places. However, for pure exhilaration, as self-appointed co-pilot and navigator for that steaming giant as we thundered through those sleeping flatlands at 100 miles an hour . . . that remains the most memorable ride of my life.

At that water hole somewhere south of Chicago, the engineer asked, would I send him a ball with my signature on it? He wrote his name and address on a Camel wrapper.

When, moments later I arrived back at our press car and rapped on the window, Roscoe (New York *Times*) McGowen peered out before returning to his poker hand. Frantic, I rattled the window with pebbles until Bob (New York *Herald Tribune*) Cooke threw down his cards.

"Good Lord!" I said as I stormed down the aisle. "Can't you guys recognize a friendly face?"

"Good God!" honked Eddie (New York *Mirror*) Zeltner, "take a look in the mirror."

No minstrel man was ever blacker.

P.S. I still recall the message I scrawled on the ball I mailed to that address in East St. Louis: For Rex Riley, "King of the Road," from your pal Ernie Koy.

4. The Babe's Last Spikes, late September 1938—It was after a Sunday doubleheader at Ebbets Field. The Dodger locker room was full of confusion as the players scrambled to get away. Disillusioned with his role as a

"white elephant," first-base coach for Larry MacPhail's sixth-place menagerie, a strangely quiet Babe Ruth was tossing his gear into his locker when he spotted me.

"Kid," he gruffed, "what size shoe do you wear?"

"Nine-and-a-half C," I replied. "Why?"

"Same as me," commented Babe . . . and he handed me his spikes. "Even if you don't use 'em, maybe some day you'll have a kid of your own. And maybe he'll grow into these."

Adjusting his famed camel's hair cap, the Babe patted a speechless cub reporter on the shoulder and walked out of baseball.

P.S. Thirty years later I presented the spikes to the Hall of Fame in Cooperstown, where today they reside with Babe's other effects.

5. NFL Championship Game at Washington, December 8, 1940—During their Saturday workout at Griffith Stadium, Chicago Bears' end John Siegal (Columbia), whom I'd played against in college, asked whom I liked.

   "The Redskins," I replied.

   "Do yourself a favor, Dave," grinned Johnny. "Bet on us. We'll murder them."

   Final score: Bears 73, Redskins 0.

   If, covering that holocaust from the press box was unforgettable, the post-game scene in the Redskins' locker room remains even more vivid. Standing against the wall beside veteran tackle Jim Barber, more urbane perhaps than his mates, I watched, flabbergasted. From quarterback Sammy Baugh down to the rawest rookie, they sobbed like beaten children, coach Ray Flaherty included.

An ex-catcher who didn't go straight, Joe Garagiola knows all the signals.

UPI

III

Batter Up

A Potpourri of 9 Lists from Joe Garagiola

25 People Who Quit the Yankees Since George Steinbrenner Bought the Team in 1973

1. Michael Burke
2. Howard Berk
3. Lee MacPhail
4. Bob Fishel
5. Ralph Houk
6. Marty Appel
7. Al Rosen
8. Tal Smith
9. Clyde Kluttz
10. George Pfister
11. Gabe Paul
12. Pat Nugent
13. Pat Gillick
14. Elliot Wahle
15. Dr. Sidney Gaynor
16. Bobby Cox
17. Mickey Morabito
18. Joseph A. W. Iglehart
19. Rob Franklin
20. Jerry Waring
21. Pam Boucher
22. Francis J. (Steve) O'Neill
23. Herman Schneider
24. Joe Garagiola, Jr.
25. Dick Howser (?)

Note: Rather than admitting this is a source of embarrassment to him, Steinbrenner insists it is a tribute to the Yankees that other clubs hire away his people. "Most of the people who left me went to bigger jobs," he says, citing Lee MacPhail, American League President; Bobby Cox, who went from a coach to manager of the Atlanta Braves; and Gabe Paul, Tal Smith, and Pat Gillick, who left the Yankees to become front-office chiefs for the Indians, Astros, and Blue Jays.

3 QUESTIONS MOST OFTEN ASKED OF NBC "GAME OF THE WEEK" ANNOUNCERS BY FANS

1. Is this the Game of the Week?
2. Are you going to broadcast this game?
3. Why do you have so many American League games? (If National League City. If we are in an American League city, it's "Why do you have so many National League games?)

3 QUESTIONS OFTEN ASKED OF NBC "GAME OF THE WEEK" ANNOUNCERS BY PLAYERS

1. Will you say hello to my ______ ? (Fill in the blank with wife, father, mother, son, daughter, grandfather, grandmother, former coach, or all of them.)
2. Will this game be seen in ______ ? (Fill in home town.)
3. What did you mean when you were talking about me and you said ________ ?

3 QUESTIONS MOST OFTEN ASKED OF NBC "GAME OF THE WEEK" ANNOUNCERS BY UMPIRES

1. You guys and your #$%&@? replays, why don't you take them and ______ ?
2. You guys and your #$%&@? replays, why don't you take them and ______ ?
3. You guys and your #$%&@? replays, why don't you take them and ______ ?

3 BEST ON-CAMERA LINE-UP GIVERS

1. Ron Luciano (included because he was doing it as an umpire).
2. Jay Johnstone
3. Tug McGraw

3 BASEBALL PEOPLE I WOULD LIKE TO GO ON THE DISABLED LIST WITH

1. Ellis Clary—He once had a heart attack and while they were putting him into the ambulance, he asked his friend to get the mileage so he could turn it in on his expense account. Great story-teller, especially Clint Courtney stories.
2. Walter Shannon—Would remember all the players I ever played with or against and have a story about each one. This list would also include players I played with or against on the playgrounds in St. Louis.
3. Tom Lasorda—He would have unlimited stories, visits from guys like Don Rickles, Pat Henry, and I know I would be eating good.

4 INTERVIEWS I WOULD LIKE TO SEE AND HEAR (YOUR CHOICE AS TO INTERVIEWER)

1. Billy Martin and George Steinbrenner
2. Earl Weaver and Ron Luciano
3. Dave Kingman and Steve Carlton
4. Charley Finley and Bowie Kuhn

3 SLOPPIEST TOBACCO CHEWERS

1. Danny Murtaugh—After sitting next to him, you walked away looking like you had measles.
2. Don Zimmer—Makes you a meteorologist, you can't sit downwind of him.
3. Yogi Berra—Talks in a light drizzle.

3 BEST HITTING ADVISERS

1. Stan Musial—On hitting the spitball: "Hit the dry side."
2. Ralph Garr—Clyde King said of him, "Some players hit the ball where it is pitched, he hits it IF it is pitched."

3. Harmon Killebrew—On how to hit the knuckleball: "Look for the seams and then hit in-between them."

MY 3 FAVORITE LINES FROM FANS

1. Didn't you use to do something?
2. Remember me, I was in the Army with you. (I always hear this one around World Series time. The only two Army guys who never called were Eisenhower and MacArthur.)
3. I remember you with the Gashouse Gang. (Honest, I was still in school.)

Ernie Harwell's 10 Things Sure To Happen During a Baseball Rain Delay

Ernie Harwell, broadcaster for the Detroit Tigers and one of the premier baseball announcers in the business, has been watching the activity of fans over four decades of rain delays.

1. Everybody will desert the box seat area, but three kids with plastic over their heads will remain there throughout the rain.
2. The organist will play "Raindrops Keep Falling on My Head," "Singing In the Rain," and four other rain songs.
3. A banner in the center field bleachers will become so soaked that all the lettering will run together.
4. A rookie utility infielder will hope for more rain, so he can attend a downtown movie.
5. Three young ladies will run to the box seat section and try to talk with some of the players in the home dugout. The players will ignore them, but the batboy will make points.
6. Four or five players will stay in each dugout. At least one player in each dugout will be fondling a bat.
7. Two sports writers will locate a well-endowed young lady in the stands and train binoculars on her.
8. Another writer will re-visit the press room to devour two more ham and cheese sandwiches.

Broadcaster Ernie Harwell was master of ceremonies at "Ted Williams' Night" at Baltimore's Memorial Stadium in the late 1950s.

Ted Patterson Collection

9. A youngster will dash from the stands onto the field and slide on the tarp.
10. At the height of the downpour some loud-mouth fan will yell, at nobody in particular, "Play Ball!"

Ernie Harwell's 10 Goofiest Baseball Trades

1. Chattanooga shortstop Johnny Jones was traded to Charlotte, N.C., for a Thanksgiving turkey.
2. Canton, Ohio, peddled the great Cy Young to Cleveland for a suit of clothes.
3. The Red Sox sent Babe Ruth to the Yankees for a mort-

gage on Fenway Park.

4. The Detroit Tigers paid their spring training rent to Augusta, Ga., by leaving Ed Cicotte with the Augusta team.
5. Lefty Grove moved from Martinsburg, W. Va., to Baltimore in exchange for a center field fence.
6. Dallas sent pitcher Joe Martina to New Orleans in exchange for two barrels of oysters.
7. First baseman Jack Fenton went from San Francisco to the Memphis team for a box of prunes.
8. Nashville's Larry Gilbert gave up a set of golf clubs to obtain catcher Greek George.
9. In 1944, as part-owner and pitcher for Little Rock, Willis Hudlin sold himself to the Browns. After the Browns had won the pennant and Hudlin had received a World Series share, owner Hudlin re-purchased pitcher Hudlin for a cheaper price and kept the change.
10. Montreal catcher Cliff Dapper was traded to the Atlanta Crackers for baseball announcer Ernie Harwell.

Dave Newhouse's Major League All-Star Team of Players Who Grew Up in Oakland

Dave Newhouse is sports columnist for the Oakland *Tribune*.

1b	Ferris Fain
2b	Joe Morgan
3b	Cookie Lavagetto
ss	Bill Rigney
of	Frank Robinson
of	Vada Pinson
of	Curt Flood
c	Ernie Lombardi
p	Ray Kremer
p	Rudy May

Frank Robinson, a product of Oakland, dons his magistrate's wig as judge at the locker room trials when he played for the Baltimore Orioles.

UPI

Bill Parrillo's All-Time All-Star Baseball Team from Poor Little Rhode Island

Born and raised in Rhode Island, Bill Parrillo is sports columnist for the Providence *Journal*.

Catcher—Gabby Hartnett, Woonsocket
First base—Jack Flynn, Providence

Second base—Napoleon Lajoie, Woonsocket
Third base—Johnny Goryl, Cumberland
Shortstop—Jimmy (Scoops) Cooney, Cranston
Outfield—Hugh Duffy, Cranston
Outfield—Johnny Cooney, Cranston
Outfield—Joe Connolly, North Smithfield
Designated hitter— Davey Lopes, East Providence
Pitcher—Andy Coakley, Providence
Pitcher—Max Surkont, Central Falls
Pitcher—Chet Nichols, Pawtucket
Pitcher—Dave Stenhouse, Westerly
Pitcher—Phil Paine, Chepachet
Relief pitcher—Clem Labine, Lincoln
Manager—Eddie Sawyer, Westerly
General Manager—Roland Hemond, Central Falls, or Lou Gorman, Providence

Parrillo notes: "My team has three Hall of Famers (Hartnett, Lajoie, Duffy) and even comes equipped with its own umpires —Hank Soar, Pawtucket; Paul Pryor, Woonsocket; Bob Stewart, Cumberland; Jim Duffy, Pawtucket; and its own agents—Jerry Kapstein, Providence (Steve Garvey, Fred Lynn, Carlton Fisk, Joe Rudi, etc.) and Tony Pennacchia, Cranston (Jim Rice, Cecil Cooper, Butch Hobson, etc.).

"Did you know that the very first World Series was played in Rhode Island? In 1884, the Providence Grays of the National League met the New York Metropolitans of the American Association. The series was a result of an agreement signed by warring leagues to stop the raiding of players. It was a three-game series. Old Hoss Radbourne pitched all three victories for the champion Grays. And you thought Rhode Island is known just for Johnnycakes (clam cakes), the America's Cup, and Marvin Barnes."

10 Greatest Baseball Players from Georgia

Selected by Furman Bisher, sports editor and columnist of the Atlanta *Journal.*

1. Ty Cobb
2. Luke Appling

Ty Cobb, the Georgia Peach, enjoyed hunting during the off-season.

UPI

3. Johnny Mize
4. Spud Chandler
5. Cecil Travis
6. Whitlow Wyatt
7. Jim Hearn
8. Marty Marion
9. Erskine Mayer
10. Nap Rucker

Ray Fitzgerald's 50 Ways to Ease the Tension of a Baseball Strike

Ray Fitzgerald eases his tension by writing interesting, imaginative columns like this for the Boston *Globe*.

1. Set fire to a cat.
2. Write 500 times on a blackboard: "Rennie Stennett makes $260,000 a year and I don't."
3. Start a dice baseball league and appoint yourself commissioner.
4. Investigate a library.
5. Go see a soccer game.
6. Phone Charlie Finley and tell him how much you miss his mule.
7. Walk in the rain.
8. Start a charm school and name it after Dave Kingman.
9. Take out the garbage without being asked.
10. Buy a ladder and dunk a basketball.
11. Send a hand grenade to Woody Hayes.
12. Crochet a "God Bless Our Home and Marvin Miller" sampler.
13. Admire a sunset.
14. Learn how to kick a spiral.
15. Teach your dog to bunt.
16. Rearrange your baseball cards in alphabetical order.
17. Challenge A. J. Foyt to a race.
18. Re-read your collection of *Hardy Boys* books.
19. Pick somebody's pocket.
20. Hold hands with Rosie Ruiz and run 26 miles, 385 yards.
21. Try to get McCartney, Harrison, and Starr together one last time.
22. On your lunch break, practice the Statue of Liberty play with a close friend.
23. Whistle "Dixie."
24. Hit 'em where they ain't.
25. Walk a mile in somebody else's shoes.
26. Feed a ballpark hot dog to a pigeon.
27. Feed a pigeon to a ballpark hot dog.
28. Dust off your Rod Kanehl scrapbook.

29. Play hit the bat with your favorite uncle.
30. Hug a wimp.
31. Put a card in the window calling for 50 pounds of ice.
32. Skip a flat stone across a millpond.
33. Steal a base.
34. Take an agent to lunch.
35. Let an agent take you to lunch.
36. Practice chewing gum and walking at the same time.
37. Trade a cat's eye for a moonie.
38. Count the stitches on a baseball.
39. Play out your option.
40. Wiggle your ears in church.
41. Catch a tuna.
42. Fly to Disney World and throw a gum wrapper on the sidewalk.
43. Eat a hockey puck for breakfast.
44. Knit a tennis racquet.
45. Share a marshmallow with Billy Martin.
46. Sharpen your double runners.
47. Play handball in 5 o'clock traffic.
48. Make root beer in your cellar.
49. Stuff a basketball with Fettuccine Alfredo.
50. Weep for sports the way they used to be.

Joe Reichler's All-Time All-Star World Series Team

Joe Reichler, Special Assistant to Baseball Commissioner Bowie Kuhn, for many years was baseball editor of the Associated Press.

First base—Lou Gehrig, Yankees
Second base—Frank Frisch, Giants and Cardinals
Third base—Frank (Home Run) Baker, Athletics and Yankees
Shortstop—PeeWee Reese, Dodgers
Left field—Lou Brock, Cardinals
Center field—Pepper Martin, Cardinals
Right field—Babe Ruth, Yankees

Catcher—Yogi Berra, Yankees
Right-handed pitcher—Bob Gibson, Cardinals
Left-handed pitcher—Whitey Ford, Yankees

SOURCE: *The World Series* (Simon & Schuster).

Stan Musial's All-Time National League Team

First base—Bill Terry
Second base—Rogers Hornsby
Shortstop—Honus Wagner
Third base—Eddie Mathews
Left field—Henry Aaron
Center field—Willie Mays
Right field—Roberto Clemente
Catcher—Roy Campanella

Ron Luciano still calls 'em as he sees 'em.
NBC/Sports Photo Source

Pitchers—Bob Gibson
Tom Seaver
Christy Mathewson
Grover Cleveland Alexander
Carl Hubbell
Warren Spahn
Sandy Koufax
Elroy Face
Clem Labine

SOURCE: *The Complete Handbook of Baseball* (NAL, 1976).

Ron Luciano's "5 Toughest Managers I Had To Deal With"

Before becoming a commentator for NBC's "Major League Game of the Week," Ron Luciano was a colorful American League umpire.

1. Earl Weaver
2. Earl Weaver
3. Earl Weaver
4. Earl Weaver
5. Frank Robinson—"He's Earl's protégé."

Says Luciano: "The problem with Earl is that he holds a grudge. Other managers, if they disagree with a call, may holler and shout, but you can still go out for a beer with them after the game. Not Weaver. He never forgets. Heck, he even holds your minor league record against you. Once, a couple of years ago, I made a controversial call at the plate. Earl charged out of the dugout, screaming that that was the same call I'd blown at Elmira in '66. That sort of thing can get to you."

SOURCE: *Inside Sports.*

Dr. Donald S. Teig's "10 Ballplayers I Have Tested with the Best Eyes for Hitting; 10 Ballplayers I Have Tested with the Best Eyes for Pitching; and 10 Ballplayers I Have Tested Who Are Mixed Dominant"*

Dr. Donald S. Teig, an optometrist from Ridgefield, Conn., conducted a study of 275 ballplayers for Bausch & Lomb's Council on Sports Vision. "But, doc, what can you do to help me hit the curve ball?"

HITTING

1. Steve Garvey
2. Willie Mays Aikens
3. George Brett
4. Chet Lemon
5. Bob Molinaro
6. Rico Carty
7. Dale Murphy
8. Gary Mathews
9. Bruce Bochte
10. Tom Paciorek

PITCHING

1. Nolan Ryan
2. Joe Sambito
3. Larry Gura
4. Dan Quisenberry
5. Bob Welch
6. Floyd Bannister
7. Joe Niekro
8. Rich Dotson
9. Steve Busby
10. Jesse Jefferson

MIXED DOMINANT*

1. Terry Puhl
2. Chris Chambliss
3. John Mayberry
4. Claudell Washington
5. Lamar Johnson
6. Dan Meyer
7. Willie Mays Aikens
8. George Brett
9. Hal McRae
10. Willie Wilson

* Aims with left eye and bats right-handed, or aims with right eye and bats left-handed.

Note: Tests included eyesight, depth perception, eye concentration and reaction time, night vision, glare vision, peripheral vision, and eye health.

18 People Not to Invite to a Bowie Kuhn Testimonial

1. Curt Flood
2. Bill Veeck
3. Edward DeBartolo
4. Ted Turner
5. Marvin Miller
6. Mike Marshall
7. George Steinbrenner
8. Denny McLain
9. Jerold Hoffberger
10. Red Smith
11. Willie Mays
12. Hank Aaron
13. Billy Cannon, Jr.
14. Ray Kroc
15. Charlie Finley
16. Murray Chass
17. Jerome Holtzman
18. Melissa Ludtke Lincoln

Baseball's 5 Biggest Bonus Baby Flops

1. Billy Joe Davidson—The Cleveland Indians paid a reported $120,000 to sign Billy Joe after an outstanding high school career in which he averaged almost 18 strikeouts a game. Davidson never made it to the majors. The highest level of professional baseball he reached was Cedar Rapids, a class B club, where his record was 1-5.
2. Bob Taylor—The Milwaukee Braves shelled out $100,000 for this promising young catcher who batted .218 in 724 major league games over 11 seasons.
3. Frank Baumann—The Boston Red Sox reportedly paid $125,000 for this hot prospect who won 45 games in 11 seasons.
4. Bobby Guindon—The Red Sox paid $125,000 for this budding star. Guindon appeared in five games in 1964. He went one-for-eight, a .125 average, and struck out four times.
5. Paul Pettit—In January of 1950, the Pittsburgh Pirates paid $100,000 for this young pitcher. Pettit made brief appearances in 1951 and 1953. His career stats are 1-2, a 7.34 ERA, 21 walks, 14 strikeouts in 30 2/3 innings.

SOURCE: Jeff C. Young, Lebanon, Ind.

Baby-faced PeeWee Reese was one of the Dodger Boys of Summer.
Bill Greene/Sports Photo Source

PeeWee Reese's 10 Baseball Tips for Little Leaguers and Any Big Leaguers Who Didn't Learn Their Lessons

PeeWee Reese, former marbles champ in Louisville and for a span of nearly 20 years a nonpareil shortstop for the Dodgers, is a good-will ambassador for Hillerich and Bradsby, maker of the Louisville Slugger.

1. Pitchers: Keep your eye on the target until the ball is in the catcher's glove or hits the bat.
2. Pitchers: Hide the ball with your glove and body to avoid tipping off your pitches.
3. Select a bat that isn't too heavy to handle and take a comfortable stance.
4. Outfielders: Throw overhand and always one base ahead of the runner.
5. Get in front of the ball with your body and glove close to the ground for grounders.
6. Catchers: Provide a target at all times and keep it until the pitch is released.
7. Hit the ball where it is pitched. Don't try to pull a pitch that is outside.
8. When batting, keep your feet planted, elbows away from the body, shoulders level.
9. When rounding the bases, always touch the bag on the inside corner to save ground.
10. Don't try to hit home runs. Just make contact. The homers will come.

SOURCE: *The Family TV Baseball Handbook*

Herman L. Masin's All-Time Team of Players Who Won an MVP Award But Are Not in the Hall of Fame

1b—Dolph Camilli
2b—Nellie Fox
3b—Ken Boyer
ss—Phil Rizzuto
of—Roger Maris
of—Hank Sauer
of—Jackie Jensen
c—Ernie Lombardi
p—Bucky Walters

Fred Patek stood tall for nine years as the Royals' shortstop.

Malcolm Emmons

Herman L. Masin's All-Time Team of Players Who Are in the Hall of Fame, But Never Won an MVP Award

1b—Jim Bottomley
2b—Billy Herman
3b—Eddie Mathews
ss—Luke Appling
of—Goose Goslin
of—Duke Snider
of—Chick Hafey
c—Al Lopez
p—Red Ruffing

9 Players Over Whom Five-Foot, Five-Inch Fred Patek Could Tower

1. Nin Alexander, 5′2″
2. Pompeyo (Yo-Yo) Davalillo, 5′3″
3. Stubby Magner, 5′3″
4. Lou Sylvester, 5′3″
5. Monk Cline, 5′4″

J.R. Richard dwarfed all who faced him.
Rich Pilling

6. Doc Gautreau, 5'4"
7. Hugh Nicol, 5'4"
8. Ernie Oravetz, 5'4"
9. Wee Willie Keeler, 5'4½"

Jeff C. Young's All-Time Tall (6'2" or Over) and All-Time Short (5'9' or Under) Baseball Teams

TALL

First base—Willie McCovey, 6'4"
Second base—Ken Hubbs, 6'2"
Shortstop—Tony Kubek, 6'3"
Third base—Frank Thomas, 6'3"
Outfield—Dave Parker, 6'5"
Outfield—Hank Greenberg, 6'3½"
Outfield—Ted Williams, 6'3"
Catcher—GusTriandos, 6'3"
Designated hitter— Frank Howard, 6'7"
Right-handed pitcher—J. R. Richard, 6'8"
Left-handed pitcher—Steve Carlton, 6'5"
Relief pitcher—Rollie Fingers, 6'4"
Manager—Dallas Green, 6'5"

SHORT

First base—George Kell, 5'9"
Second base—Joe Morgan, 5'7"
Shortstop—Fred Patek, 5'5"
Third base—Tommy Harper, 5'9"
Outfield—Wee Willie Keeler, 5'4½"
Outfield—Pepper Martin, 5'8"
Outfield—Paul Waner, 5'8½"
Catcher—Yogi Berra, 5'7½"
Designated hitter— Mel Ott, 5'9"
Right-handed pitcher—Joe Bush, 5'9"
Left-handed pitcher—Bobby Shantz, 5'9"
Relief pitcher—Roy Face, 5'8"
Manager—John McGraw, 5'7"
Honorable Mention—Eddie Gaedel, 3'7"

Note: George Kell was primarily a third baseman, but he did play 85 games at first. "It's very tough finding a first baseman 5'9" or under," says Jeff Young, who sizes them up from his home in Lebanon, Indiana.

10 Tragedies To Befall the California Angels

1. In 1961, Johnny James, a promising young pitcher acquired from the Yankees, throws a curve ball and feels something snap in his arm. He has broken a bone. He never pitches again.
2. In 1964, Ken McBride, the ace of the Angels' pitching staff, is driving his automobile and is struck from the rear. He suffers whiplash injuries to his back and neck and wins only four more games in the big leagues.
3. In 1965, rookie Dick Wantz is the surprise of the Angels' spring training camp. Stardom seems inevitable. Within four months, he is dead of a brain tumor at age 25.
4. In 1968, Angels' relief pitcher Minnie Rojas tries to pass a truck on the highway and collides with an oncoming car. His spinal cord is severed and he is permanently paralyzed.
5. In 1969, Tom Egan, the Angels' No. 1 catcher, is struck in the eye by an Earl Wilson fastball. He is carried off the field on a stretcher and never completely regains his sight.
6. In 1973, shortstop Bobby Valentine, one of baseball's brightest young stars, is sent to centerfield to replace Ken Berry. He crashes into the outfield wall, breaks his right leg and never is the same again.
7. In 1974, rookie Bruce Heinbechner is destined to be the Angels' left-handed relief specialist. Shortly before the season opens, he is killed in an auto accident, half a mile from the team's hotel.
8. In 1977, Mike Miley, ticketed to be the Angels' starting shortstop, drives his sports car off the road and is killed.
9. In 1978, Lyman Bostock flees the Minnesota Twins and signs a $2.3 million contract with the Angels. In September, he is shot and killed while riding in a car with family and friends in Gary, Ind.

The itinerant Bobo Newsom as a St. Louis Brown in 1938. *UPI*

10. In 1980, Bruce Kison signs a $2.4 million contract and is supposed to replace Nolan Ryan. Instead, he undergoes major arm surgery and the Angels collapse in their bid to repeat as American League West champs.

Submitted by Jim Hawkins, sports columnist of the Detroit *Free Press.*

5 Most-Traded Baseball Players

1. Bobo Newsom—16 times
2. Tommy Davis—11 times
3. John Joseph Doyle—10 times
4. Deacon McGuire—10 times
5. Bob Miller—10 times

SOURCE: Philadelphia *Inquirer*.

Ray Robinson's All-Time College Baseball Team

Ray Robinson is a Columbia man who had one time at bat in a freshman baseball game. Needless to say, he struck out. He is currently Executive Editor of *Seventeen* magazine.

First base—Lou Gehrig, Columbia; George Sisler, Michigan.
Second base—Frank Frisch, Fordham; Eddie Collins, Columbia; Charlie Gehringer, Michigan; Jackie Robinson, UCLA.
Third base—Red Rolfe, Dartmouth; Mike Schmidt, Ohio U.
Shortstop—Lou Boudreau, Illinois; Dick Groat, Duke; Alvin Dark, LSU.
Outfield—Hank Greenberg, NYU; Reggie Jackson, Arizona State; Riggs Stephenson, Alabama; Harry Hooper, St. Mary's; Sam Chapman, California.
Cather—Mickey Cochrane, Boston U.
Pitchers—Christy Mathewson, Bucknell; Sandy Koufax, Cincinnati; Ted Lyons, Baylor; Bob Gibson, Creighton; Tom Seaver, USC; Robin Roberts, Michigan State; Johnny Murphy, Fordham; Mike Marshall, Michigan State; Jim Konstanty, Syracuse.
Subs—Bill White, Hiram; Billy Werber, Duke; Burgess Whitehead, North Carolina; Jeff Torborg, Rutgers; Sal Bando, Arizona State.
Bench savant—Moe Berg, Princeton.
Manager—Miller Huggins, Cincinnati.
General Manager—Branch Rickey, Ohio Wesleyan.
Harvard Men—Charlie Devens, Ulysses (Tony) Lupien.

Joe McCarthy's 10 Commandments for Success in the Majors

Marse Joe McCarthy managed in the major leagues for 24 years with the Cubs, Yankees, and Red Sox, from 1926 through 1950. He won 3,489 games and lost 1,335 and his winning percentage of .614 was the best in baseball history. In nine World Series, he won 43 games and lost 30, for a winning percentage of .698.

1. Nobody ever became a ballplayer by walking after a ball.
2. You will never become a .300 hitter unless you take the bat off your shoulder.
3. An outfielder who throws in back of a runner is locking the barn after the horse is stolen.
4. Keep your head up and you may not have to keep it down.
5. When you start to slide, slide. He who changes his mind may have to change a good leg for a bad one.
6. Do not alibi on bad hops. Anybody can field the good ones.
7. Always run them out. You never can tell.
8. Do not quit.
9. Do not fight too much with the umpires. You cannot expect them to be as perfect as you are.
10. A pitcher who hasn't control hasn't anything.

Johnny Bench's 6 Toughest Base Stealers

1. Davey Lopes—"Great quickness and acceleration. He runs on dirt in L.A., which is tough."
2. Ron LeFlore—"He was new to the National League in 1980, and now he's back in the American League. I won't miss him."
3. Omar Moreno—"Runs with the best. Acceleration, long strides and a long headfirst slide are what make him tough to catch."

Once on base, there is no stopping Ron LeFlore.

Rich Pilling

4. Cesar Cedeno—"His knees are his only question marks. Healthy, he'll run with anyone."
5. Joe Morgan—"Again, his legs are a problem. But when you need a stolen base, he'll get it for you."
6. Rudy Law—"Young, but he'll soon be a top threat."

Note: This list is not in order of toughness. "They're all tough," says Bench.

SOURCE: *Inside Sports.*

9 Players Who Batted 1.000 for Their Major League Careers

1. Steve Biras, Cleveland, 1944, two at-bats
2. Roy Gleason, Los Angeles (N), 1963, one at-bat
3. Mike Hopkins, Pittsburgh, 1902, two at-bats
4. Steve Kuczek, Boston (N), 1949, one at-bat
5. Chuck Lindstrom, Chicago (A), 1958, one at-bat
6. Red Lutz, Cincinnati, 1922, one at-bat
7. John Paciorek, Houston, 1963, three at-bats
8. Fred Schemanske, Washington, 1923, two at-bats
9. Allie Watt, Washington, 1920, one at-bat

Note: Chuck Lindstrom is the son of Hall of Famer Freddie Lindstrom, and John Paciorek is the brother of major league Tom Paciorek.

9 Pitchers Who Pitched Only One-Third of an Inning in the Major Leagues

1. Eddie Ainsmith, Washington, 1913
2. Ted Cather, St. Louis (N), 1913
3. Joe Cleary, Washington, 1945
4. Marc Filley, Washington, 1934
5. Fritz Fisher, Detroit, 1964
6. Art Goodwin, New York (A), 1905
7. Harley Grossman, Washington, 1952
8. Jim Mosolf, Pittsburgh, 1930
9. Frank Wurm, Brooklyn, 1944

7 Pitchers Who Never Got Anybody Out in Their Major League Careers

1. Joe Brown, Chicago (A), 1927
2. Fred Bruckbauer, Minnesota, 1961
3. Doc Hamann, Cleveland, 1922
4. Willis Koenigmark, St. Louis (N), 1919
5. Bill Moore, Detroit, 1925
6. Mike Palagyi, Washington, 1939
7. Jim Schelle, Philadelphia (A), 1939

12 Sluggers Who Hit 60 or More Home Runs in a Single Season

	No	Team	League	Year
1. Joe Bauman	72	Roswell	Longhorn	1954
2. Joe Hauser	69	Minneapolis	Amer. Assn.	1933
3. Bob Crues	69	Amarillo	West Texas-N.M.	1948
4. Dick Stuart	66	Lincoln	Western	1956
5. Bob Lennon	64	Nashville	Southern	1954
6. Joe Hauser	63	Baltimore	International	1930
7. Moose Clabaugh	62	Tyler	East Texas	1926
8. Ken Guettler	62	Shreveport	Texas	1956
9. Roger Maris	61	New York	American	1961
10. Babe Ruth	60	New York	American	1927
11. Tony Lazzeri	60	Salt Lk. City	Pacific Coast	1925
12. Frosty Kennedy	60	Plainview	Southwest	1956

16 Players Who Had More RBIs Than Games Played (Through 1980)

Player	Year
1. Babe Ruth	1921, 1927, 1929, 1930, 1931, 1932
2. Lou Gehrig	1927, 1930, 1931, 1934, 1937
3. Jimmie Foxx	1930, 1932, 1933, 1938
4. Joe DiMaggio	1937, 1939, 1940, 1948
5. Al Simmons	1927, 1929, 1930
6. Hank Greenberg	1935, 1937, 1940
7. Ken Williams	1922, 1925
8. Hack Wilson	1929, 1930
9. Rogers Hornsby	1925
10. Mel Ott	1929
11. Chuck Klein	1930
12. Hal Trosky	1936
13. Vern Stephens	1949
14. Ted Williams	1949
15. Walt Dropo	1950
16. George Brett	1980

SOURCE: National Baseball Hall of Fame and Museum.

Babe Ruth went into training for his contract bout with Yankee owner Colonel Jacob Ruppert in 1933.

UPI

15 Greatest Home Run Hitters of All-Time Per 100 At-Bats (Through 1980)

Player	*Home Runs Per 100 ABs*
1. Babe Ruth	8.5
2. Ralph Kiner	7.1
3. Harmon Killebrew	7.0

4.	Dave Kingman	7.0
5.	Ted Williams	6.8
6.	Mike Schmidt	6.6
7.	Mickey Mantle	6.6
8.	Jimmie Foxx	6.6
9.	Hank Greenberg	6.4
10.	Willie McCovey	6.4
11.	Lou Gehrig	6.2
12.	Hank Aaron	6.1
13.	Willie Mays	6.1
14.	Willie Stargell	6.1
15.	Eddie Mathews	6.0

SOURCE: National Baseball Hall of Fame and Museum.

No other third baseman has hit as much as George Brett's .390 in 1980.

Mitchell B. Reibel

All-Time Team with Highest Single-Season Batting Averages at Each Position (Through 1980)

AMERICAN LEAGUE

1b	George Sisler, 1922 (.420)
2b	Napoleon Lajoie, 1901 (.422)
3b	George Brett, 1980 (.390)
ss	Luke Appling, 1936 (.388)
of	Ty Cobb, 1911 (.420)
c	Bill Dickey, 1936 (.362)
p	Walter Johnson, 1925 (.433)

NATIONAL LEAGUE

1b	Bill Terry, 1930 (.401)
2b	Rogers Hornsby, 1924 (.424)
3b	Fred Lindstrom, 1930 (.379)
ss	Arky Vaughan, 1935 (.385)
of	Lefty O'Doul, 1929 (.398)
c	Chief Meyers, 1912 (.358)
p	Jack Bentley, 1923 (.427)

SOURCE: National Baseball Hall of Fame and Museum.

50 Baseball Players with Career Batting Averages Under .220 for a Minimum of 1,000 At-Bats (Through 1980)

Player	*At-Bats*	*Average*
1. Bill Bergen	3028	.170
2. Ray Oyler	1265	.175
3. Fritz Buelow	1299	.189
4. Mike Ryan	1920	.193
5. Jose Morales	1053	.195
6. Sam Agnew	1537	.204

7.	Billy Sullivan	3345	.207
8.	John Henry	1920	.207
9.	Jackie Hernandez	1480	.208
10.	Gabby Street	1501	.208
11.	Luke Boone	1028	.209
12.	Tom Needham	1491	.209
13.	Luis Gomez	1216	.211
14.	Jack Heidemann	1093	.211
15.	Terry Humphrey	1055	.211
16.	Dave Nicholson	1419	.212
17.	Mike Powers	1782	.212
18.	Dave Campbell	1252	.213
19.	Jerry Kindall	2057	.213
20.	Red Kleinow	1665	.213
21.	Harry Smith	1004	.213
22.	Dick Tracewski	1231	.213
23.	Mario Mendoza	1091	.213
24.	Luis Alvarado	1160	.214
25.	Lena Blackburne	1807	.214
26.	Dave Duncan	2885	.214
27.	Jeff Torborg	1391	.214
28.	Phil Roof	2151	.215
29.	Rusty Torres	1242	.215
30.	Bobby Wine	3172	.215
31.	Ray Berres	1330	.216
32.	Hunter Hill	1200	.216
33.	Hector Torres	1738	.216
34.	Walter Blair	1255	.217
35.	Vic Harris	1610	.217
36.	Ted Kazanski	1329	.217
37.	Clyde Manion	1153	.217
38.	Dal Maxvill	3443	.217
39.	Wes Westrum	2322	.217
40.	Doc White	1279	.217
41.	George McBride	5526	.218
42.	Fred Raymer	1380	.218
43.	John Boccabella	1462	.219
44.	Harry Howell	1263	.219
45.	Billy Hunter	1875	.219
46.	Mike Kahoe	1088	.219

47. Lou Ritter	1437	.219
48. Jimmy Smith	1127	.219
49. Skeeter Webb	2274	.219
50. Al Weis	1578	.219

SOURCE: Bob Rosen, Elias Sports Bureau, who says, "The list is limited to non-pitchers and only records from 1901 were used. (Editor's note: 1901 begins the modern era of baseball.) If a player appeared prior to 1901, only his figures compiled from 1901 on were used."

Rosen also notes that hitting improved in 1930 and began to decline in the '60s. It should also be pointed out that the 50 men listed obviously had some skill to have stayed in the major leagues long enough to acquire 1,000 at-bats. Many were defensive specialists, and catchers and shortstops, in particular, dominate the list.

Note: The Jose Morales listed played with Oakland and Montreal in the 1970s and is not the same Jose Morales who batted .303 for Minnesota in 1980.

Keith Olbermann's 42 Greatest World Series Flops, Obscure Heroes, Fielding Performances, Controversies, and Upsets

FLOPS

1. Ted Williams, 1946—A .342 hitter in the regular season, Williams batted .200 against the Cardinals, five weak singles and one RBI, and popped out with the lead run on second and two out in the final game.
2. Honus Wagner, 1903—Hobbled by injury, the all-time great shortstop batted only .222, went hitless over the last three games, and made six errors as the Pirates lost to the Red Sox.
3. Babe Ruth, 1922—His great Series were yet to come when the Babe got only two hits in 17 at-bats and drove in just one run as the Giants swept the Yankees.
4. Gil Hodges, 1952—They prayed for Gil Hodges in Brooklyn churches as the Dodger first baseman suffered through 21 hitless at-bats in the Series defeat to the hated Yankees.

5. Eddie Murray, 1979—After going four-for-five in the first two games, the Oriole first baseman went hitless in his next 21 at-bats against the Pirates, the last out coming with the bases loaded, two out, and the Pirates leading, 2-1, in the eighth inning of Game 7.
6. Bob Feller, 1948—After waiting 12 years to pitch in the World Series, Feller lost both of his starts to the Braves, the only games the Indians lost. He was nipped, 1-0, in the opener, then suffered the humiliation of being tattooed for seven runs in an 11-5 defeat before 86,000 fans in Cleveland in Game 5.
7. Roger Peckinpaugh, 1925—The American League's MVP during the regular season, the Senator shortstop made eight errors in the Series against Pittsburgh, his errors setting up the winning run in Game 2, two of the three Pirates runs in Game 6, and the winning run in Game 7.
8. Hugh Casey, 1941—The famous "dropped third strike" of Game 4 of the 1941 World Series is generally blamed on Dodger catcher Mickey Owen, but the four runs the Yankees scored after the play were the work of ace reliever Casey, who absorbed two defeats in the Series won by the Yankees in five games.
9. Dick Sisler, 1950—His three-run homer in the 10th inning won the final game of the season and put the Phillies in the Series, but he would get only one hit in the four-game sweep by the Yankees, batting .059.
10. Jimmy Sheckard, 1906—Long before Gil Hodges, Sheckard was hitless in 21 at bats as his Cubs fell to the "Hitless Wonder" White Sox.

OBSCURE HEROES

1. George Rohe, 1906—Inserted by White Sox manager Fielder Jones at third base because of an injury to short-stop George Stacey Davis, Rohe tripled in the first game and scored the first run in a 2-1 victory. In game three, Rohe's bases-loaded triple gave Big Ed Walsh all the runs he needed for a 3-0 victory, and Rohe later drove in another run in the Series as the "Hitless Wonders" defeated the mighty Cubs, who had won 116 games in

This is the celebrated play in which Brooklyn's Mickey Owen missed the third strike on the Yankees' Tommy Henrich in the 1941 World Series.

UPI

the regular season. But by 1908, Rohe's big league career was over.

2. Dusty Rhodes, 1954—Pinch-hitting for Monte Irvin in Game 1, Rhodes hit a three-run homer in the ninth inning off Bob Lemon to give the Giants a 5-2 victory. In the second game, again batting for Irvin, he singled in the tying run off Early Wynn, sparking a three-run rally that gave the Giants a 3-1 victory. In Game 3, he pinch-hit for Irvin one more time and lined the first pitch for a two-run single. In six at-bats, Rhodes had four hits and seven RBI as the Giants swept the Indians.

Dusty Rhodes was the New York Giants' surprise in the 1954 World Series.

UPI

3. Babe Adams, 1909—With only 30 games of big league experience behind him, Adams pitched three complete game victories for the Pirates against the Tigers.
4. Nippy Jones, 1957—Winding down a moderately successful big league career as a pinch-hitter, Jones proved that neatness counts. Pinch-hitting for Milwaukee, Jones proved he had been hit by a pitch by insisting that umpire Augie Donatelli check the baseball for shoe polish. The ump did, awarded Jones first base, and that ignited a three-run rally in Game 4 that turned the Series with the Yankees in the Braves' favor.
5. Don Larsen, 1956—In 1954, Larsen was a 3-21 pitcher for the Orioles and was still a rather nondescript pitcher two seasons later when he recorded 27 consecutive seemingly effortless outs against the Dodgers for the only perfect game in World Series history. It was a feat Larsen milked through 1967, although he never again won more than 10 games in a season.
6. Larry Sherry, 1959—The dawn of the "ace reliever" in the World Series can be pinpointed to 1959 when Sherry, an unknown rookie, won or saved each of the Dodgers' four victories over the White Sox. To top it off, he batted .500.
7. George Whiteman, 1918—A 36-year-old utility player with only 85 big league games to his credit, Whiteman became the Red Sox cleanup hitter in the Series with the Cubs because many stars had marched off to war. In Game 1, his single set up the only run in a 1-0 victory and his two tremendous catches in left field saved the game; another leaping catch took a two-run home run away from Dode Paskert in a 2-1 victory in Game 3; and his somersaulting catch of a low liner in the eighth inning of the final game wrapped up the Series. But in making the catch, Whiteman injured his shoulder and would never play another major league game.
8. Brian Doyle, 1978—Replacing injured Willie Randolph at second base for the Yankees against the Dodgers, Doyle had recorded neither a regular season RBI nor an extra-base hit. In the Series, he led all hitters with a .438

In his typical diving manner, Baltimore's Brooks Robinson spears a Johnny Bench liner in the 1970 World Series.

UPI

average, drove in two runs, scored four and excelled in the field.

9. Pepper Martin, 1931—In his rookie season, Martin had earned the regular centerfield job with the Cardinals, but it was in the Series against the Tigers that he really ran wild, batting .500, driving in five of the Cardinals' 19 runs and stealing five bases against the great Mickey Cochrane.
10. Jimmie Wilson, 1940—Ernie Lombardi's injury and the death of Willard Hershberger forced the 40-year old Wilson out of semiretirement and into the starting catcher's job for the Reds. Wilson batted .353, stole the only base of the Series, and expertly handled the Reds' pitching staff in their Series victory over the Tigers.

FIELDING PERFORMANCES

1. Willie Mays, 1954—The most famous catch in Series history. Vivid is the picture of Mays, the No. 24 on his back squarely to the plate, hatless, gathering in over his shoulder the titanic blast hit by the Indians' Vic Wertz some 500 feet from home plate. It came in Game 1 with the score tied, 2-2, two Indians on base, and none out in the eighth inning and saved two runs in a game eventually won by the Giants, 5-2.
2. Graig Nettles, 1978—In Game 3 alone, Nettles saved at least five runs with three acrobatic stops, two with the bases loaded. The third baseman was unbelievable with eight putouts and 18 assists as the Yankees beat the Dodgers for the second straight Series.
3. Bill Wambsganss, 1920—The famed unassisted triple play, the only one in World Series history, happened as follows: With Cleveland leading, 7-0, in the fifth inning of Game 5, Pete Kilduff and Otto Miller reached base for Brooklyn. Clarence Mitchell lined a ball toward right center, but Wambsganss intercepted it, stepped on second, and chased Miller back to first, eventually tagging him for the third out.
4. Brooks Robinson, 1970—Eight years before Nettles, Robinson's play at third stymied the Reds time after time to lead the Orioles to a five-game victory.

5. Al Gionfriddo, 1947—It was perhaps the only time Joe DiMaggio showed emotion on the ballfield as he kicked dirt after watching the tiny Dodger outfielder race to the bullpen to pull down DiMaggio's home run bid with an across-the-body, twisting catch after a long run, then slamming into the bullpen fence but holding the ball. It came with two runners on in the sixth inning of Game 6 and remains as one of the greatest catches in Series history.
6. Sandy Amoros, 1955—The Dodgers, who had never won a World Series, led, 2-0, in the sixth inning of the final game. With two on, Yogi Berra hit a twisting drive into the left field corner. Off and running, little-known Dodger left fielder Sandy Amoros caught up to the ball and grabbed it in his outstretched glove, then wheeled and relayed to shortstop PeeWee Reese, whose throw to Gil Hodges doubled Gil McDougald off first to save the game and the Series.
7. Tommie Agee, 1969—Agee made not one, but two catches to save the Mets' third game victory over the Orioles. In the fourth, with the Mets leading, 3-0, and two Orioles on base, Agee raced into left center to grab Elrod Hendricks' bid for a two-run triple. Three innings later, with the bases loaded and the Mets leading 4-0, Agee caught Paul Blair's low line drive as he slid across the outfield grass on his knees.
8. Ron Swoboda, 1969—The day after Agee foiled the Orioles, Swoboda picked up the cue in the ninth inning with the Mets leading, 1-0. The Orioles had two runners on base when Brooks Robinson chipped one into shallow right. Swoboda charged the ball and caught it off his shoetops while sliding along the outfield grass. The tying run scored after the catch, but Swoboda prevented the go-ahead run from also scoring and the Mets won the game, 2-1, in the 10th.

CONTROVERSIES

1. Sam Rice's "Catch"—In the third game of the 1925 Series, the Senators led the Pirates 4-3 with two out in the eighth. Pittsburgh's Earl Smith sent a fly to right

center where Rice vaulted the outfield wall, vanished from sight, then emerged clutching the ball. Umpire Charlie Rigler ruled Rice had caught the ball, but there were doubts, and for years Rice answered the question: "Did you catch it?" with "The umpire said I did." Rice promised to confess after his death. He passed away in 1974, leaving an envelope. When opened, the envelope had a statement: "I caught it."

2. Ken Burkhardt's Out Call—In the sixth inning of the opener of the 1970 Series between the Reds and Orioles, Cincinnati's Bernie Carbo was on third when Ty Cline bounced a chopper in front of the plate. Neither plate umpire Burkhardt nor Oriole catcher Elrod Hendricks expected Carbo to try to score, so the umpire straddled the line for a "fair-foul" call and Hendricks picked up the ball with his bare hand. Suddenly, in dashed Carbo. Hendricks whirled toward the plate, but Burkhardt was in his way as the catcher tried to tag the runner. Burkhardt called Carbo out; replays and photos show Hendricks tagged Carbo, but with his empty glove, not the ball. P. S. Films also show that Carbo never touched the plate.
3. Interference or No?—After bunting to sacrifice a runner to second in the 10th inning of Game 3 of the 1975 Series between Cincinnati and Boston, the Reds' Ed Armbrister collided with Carlton Fisk as the catcher jumped out after the ball. Fisk threw wildly to set up the winning run as plate umpire Larry Barnett refused to call interference on Armbrister.
4. Zimmerman's Great Chase—The first run of the deciding game of the 1917 World Series scored in bizarre fashion. With Eddie Collins and Joe Jackson on first and third for the White Sox, Chicago's Happy Felsch hit the ball back to the Giants' pitcher, Rube Benton. Benton trapped Collins off third, but rather than throwing to his catcher to force the runner back to his base, as is the accepted fashion, Benton threw to third baseman Heinie Zimmerman. Catcher Bill Rariden left the plate unguarded as he came to aid Zimmerman in the run-down and Collins dashed past Rariden and

outran Zimmerman to the plate.

5. Nippy Jones and the Shoe Polish—The pinch-hitter convinced umpire Augie Donatelli he had been hit on the shoe with a pitch by showing the polish scuff on the baseball and that started a three-run rally that gave the Braves a victory in Game 4 of the 1957 World Series and eventual Series victory over the Yankees.
6. Cleon Jones and the Shoe Polish—Baltimore led the Mets, 3-0, in the sixth inning of Game 5 of the 1969 World Series when a Dave McNally pitch appeared to nick Cleon Jones. Umpire Lou DiMuro didn't agree, until he saw the telltale shoe polish on the ball. Jones was awarded first base and Donn Clendenon followed with a home run that started the Mets on a comeback that would win the game and the Series.
7. The Pickoff That Wasn't—The deciding run of the Boston Braves' 1-0 first game victory over Cleveland in the 1948 Series scored after a heated debate at second base between shortstop and manager Lou Boudreau of the Indians and umpire Bill Stewart. The Indians appeared to have picked Boston pinch-runner Phil Masi off the bag, but Stewart said no, and moments later Masi scored the only run of the game on a single by Tommy Holmes.
8. The Lightest Darkness—The Giants and Yankees were tied 3-3 in the 10th inning of the third game of the 1922 Series when, with light still prevailing, umpires Bill Klem and George Hildebrand called the game because of darkness. The mysterious decision was debated for 45 minutes more before the sun set that evening, and it so infuriated Commissioner Kenesaw Mountain Landis that he ordered all gate receipts turned over to charity.

UPSETS

1. White Sox Over Cubs, 1906—They had batted just .230 and hit only six homers during the season, were without their top batter and were facing a team that had won 76 percent of its games. Not surprisingly, the White Sox were given virtually no chance of beating the crosstown Cubs, yet they pulled it off in six, using sufficient pitch-

ing and the secret weapon of substitute third baseman George Rohe to stun the Cubs.

2. Orioles Over Dodgers, 1966—The Dodgers were prohibitive favorites over the Orioles, mostly on reputation and pitching (Koufax, Drysdale, Osteen). Never has a team been more completely shut down. The Dodgers scored two runs in the first game and did not score again and they never led a Series game at any time. Baltimore's Baby Birds, Jim Palmer, Wally Bunker and Dave McNally, averaging just under 22 years of age, pitched shutouts in the last three games of the shocking four-game sweep.

3. Mets Over Orioles, 1969—The hapless Mets of 1968 became the giant, or more accurately, Oriole killers of 1969 with names like Al Weis, Ron Swoboda, and J. C. Martin losing their humorous overtones and knocking off the Birds in five games, winning four straight after an opening game defeat.

4. Giants Over Indians, 1954—It is ironic that the teams with the best winning percentage in each league's history were stunningly upset in the subsequent Series. The 1954 Indians, winners of 111 games, were left at the gate by the surprising Giants, whose key ingredients were Willie Mays and pinch-hitter Dusty Rhodes, in a four-game sweep.

5. Braves Over A's, 1914—The "Miracle Braves" had been last on July 19 and many feel their rise to a Series sweep of the A's was baseball's all-time greatest upset story. But the quality of the shock must be tempered by a few facts. The A's were completely overconfident, many of the Philadelphia stars had already agreed to jump to the rival Federal League in 1915, and Boston manager George Stallings had overcome the handicap of a weak lineup by instituting the then-novel platoon system.

6. Reds Over White Sox, 1919—Little needs to be said of this first and only fixed Series won by the Reds from the "Black Sox," other than, as in all upsets, this one had a

secret ingredient—the bribes the corrupt White Sox players took to lose the Series.

SOURCE: *Baseball Magazine.*

16 Outstanding Players Who Never Played in a World Series

1. George Sisler
2. Ernie Banks
3. Ted Lyons
4. Luke Appling
5. Billy Williams
6. Addie Joss
7. Napoleon Lajoie
8. Ralph Kiner
9. Jim Bunning
10. Lindy McDaniel
11. Rod Carew
12. Ferguson Jenkins
13. Gaylord Perry
13. Phil Niekro
15. Bobby Murcer
16. Bobby Bonds

IV

Touchdown

The Top 21 NFL Games of the 1970s

1. Pittsburgh 13, Oakland 7; AFC divisional playoff, December 23, 1972—A desperation pass from Terry Bradshaw ricocheted off defender Jack Tatum into the hands of Franco Harris, the so-called "Immaculate Reception." Harris ran 42 yards to complete a 60-yard winning touchdown play with five seconds to play.
2. Miami 27, Kansas City 24; AFC divisional playoff, December 25, 1971—The NFL's longest game ended after 82 minutes and 40 seconds when Garo Yepremian kicked a 37-yard field goal at 7:40 of the second sudden-death overtime period. Larry Csonka set up Yepremian's winning kick with a 29-yard run.
3. Pittsburgh 35, Dallas 31; Super Bowl XIII, January 21, 1979—Terry Bradshaw completed 17 of 30 passes for 318 yards, a personal career high, and threw a record four touchdown passes to help Pittsburgh become the first team to win three Super Bowls.
4. Pittsburgh 31, Los Angeles 19; Super Bowl XIV, January 20, 1980—Terry Bradshaw completed 14 of 21 passes for 309 yards and set two Super Bowl passing

Super Bowl XIII featured four touchdown passes by Pittsburgh's Terry Bradshaw.
Malcolm Emmons

records as the Steelers became the first team to win four Super Bowls. Bradshaw brought Pittsburgh from behind twice in the second half against a Rams team directed by quarterback Vince Ferragamo, who completed 15 of 26 passes for 212 yards.

5. Oakland 28, Miami 26; AFC divisional playoff, December 21, 1974—Clarence Davis's fantastic catch of an eight-yard touchdown pass from Ken Stabler with 25 seconds to play gave Oakland a come-from-behind victory and snuffed out the Dolphins' hopes of a third straight Super Bowl victory. Linebacker Phil Villapiano intercepted Bob Griese's pass with 21 seconds left.
6. Dallas 17, Minnesota 14; NFC divisional playoff, December 28, 1975—Roger Staubach moved the Cowboys 85 yards out of the shotgun formation and hit Drew Pearson with a 50-yard touchdown pass as the clock showed 24 seconds remaining.
7. Dallas 30, San Francisco 28; NFC divisional playoff, December 23, 1972—Roger Staubach came off the bench and led a 17-point fourth-quarter rally, finishing the spree with a 10-yard touchdown pass to Ron Sellers with 52 seconds to play. The 49ers had capitalized on five Cowboy turnovers for a 28-13 edge going into the final period.
8. Oakland 37, Baltimore 31; AFC divisional playoff, December 24, 1977—The third-longest game in NFL history was decided by Ken Stabler's touchdown pass to Dave Casper, which came after 15:43 of overtime. The Colts' scoring included an 87-yard kickoff return by Marshall Johnson.
9. Dallas 35, Washington 34; regular season, December 16, 1979—Roger Staubach threw two scoring passes in the final four minutes, a 26-yarder to Ron Springs and a decisive 8-yarder to Tony Hill, to bring the Cowboys from a 34-21 deficit. Joe Theismann scored one touchdown and threw for another as the Redskins bowed out of playoff contention in the final game of regular-season play.
10. Pittsburgh 21, Dallas 7; Super Bowl X, January 18, 1976 —Terry Bradshaw's 64-yard touchdown pass to Lynn

Swann, followed by Glen Edwards' end zone interception, gave the Steelers their second straight Super Bowl victory. Swann set a Super Bowl record with four catches for 161 yards. Pittsburgh sacked Roger Staubach a record seven times.

11. Baltimore 16, Dallas 13; Super Bowl V, January 17, 1971—In the first Super Bowl after amalgamation of the NFL and AFL, each team had three interceptions, and there were 11 turnovers. The Colts' first touchdown came on a bizarre play when Johnny Unitas' bullet pass caromed off receiver Eddie Hinton's fingertips, off Dallas defensive back Mel Renfro, and finally to Baltimore tight end John Mackey, who rambled 45 yards to score on a 75-yard play. Jim O'Brien's 32-yard field goal with five seconds left was the clincher.
12. New Orleans 19, Detroit 17; regular season, November 8, 1970—Tom Dempsey, who was born without the front half of his right foot and no fingers on his right hand, kicked a record 63-yard field goal with two seconds remaining. Detroit had taken a 17-15 lead on Errol Mann's 18-yard field goal with 11 seconds left.
13. Oakland 31, Pittsburgh 28; regular season, September 12, 1976—Rookie Fred Steinfort's 21-yard field goal with 13 seconds remaining helped the Raiders avenge two straight AFC championship game losses to Pittsburgh. After Franco Harris's three-yard run put the Steelers on top with 6:43 left, Ken Stabler led the Raiders to three scores in the last three minutes, including a 10-yard pass to Dave Casper.
14. Dallas 24, Washington 23; regular season, November 28, 1974—Rookie quarterback Clint Longley, making his NFL debut in the third quarter because Roger Staubach was sidelined with a concussion, lofted a 50-yard pass to Drew Pearson with 23 seconds remaining, and Efren Herrera kicked the decisive extra point.
15. Houston 35, Miami 30; regular season, November 20, 1978—Earl Campbell ran for 199 yards and four touchdowns to become the NFL's ninth rookie 1,000-yard rusher. Miami's Bob Griese completed 23 of 33 passes for 349 yards, including touchdown strikes of 10 yards

to Nat Moore and 11 yards to Jimmy Cefalo.

16. Houston 26, New England 23; regular season, November 12, 1978—In an amazing comeback, the Oilers erased a 23-0 deficit. Dan Pastorini triggered the surge, completing 15 of 29 passes for 200 yards, including a game-winning 10-yard flip to Rich Caster with 2:29 left.
17. New York Jets 44, Baltimore 34; regular season, September 24, 1972—Joe Namath completed 15 of 28 passes for six touchdowns and 496 yards, the third best performance in NFL history. Rich Caster caught three of the scoring passes. Baltimore's Johnny Unitas completed 26 of 45 passes for 376 yards, his 27th 300-yard game.
18. Atlanta 14, Philadelphia 13; NFC wild-card divisional playoff, December 24, 1978—Atlanta had won four games in the last 10 seconds during the regular season. In this playoff game, the Falcons trailed 13-0 with 8:25 left and came back on Steve Bartkowski's touchdown passes of 20 yards to Jim Mitchell and 37 yards to Wallace Francis. Philadelphia's bid for a possible winning score ended when Mike Michel's 34-yard field goal try went wide with 13 seconds remaining.
19. Miami 14, Washington 7; Super Bowl VII, January 14, 1973—Don Shula's Dolphin defense permitted the Redskins to cross midfield only once in first half, and the Miami offense converted good field position into two touchdowns to complete an unprecedented 17-0 season. The Dolphins scored on a 28-yard pass from Bob Griese to Howard Twilley and a one-yard plunge by Jim Kiick, set up by Nick Buoniconti's interception of a pass by Billy Kilmer. The Redskins' only touchdown came when placekicker Garo Yepremian fumbled the ball on a pass attempt and Mike Bass ran it back for a score.
20. (tie) Oakland 24, New England 21; AFC divisional playoff, December 18, 1976—Ken Stabler rolled into the end zone for a one-yard touchdown with 10 seconds remaining to cap a 12-play, 63-yard Raider rally from a 21-10 deficit late in the third quarter.

Chicago 12, New York Giants 9; regular season,

December 18, 1977—Bob Thomas' 28-yard field goal with nine seconds to play in a freezing New Jersey rain lifted Chicago into the playoffs for the first time since 1963. Bob Avellini's passes to Greg Latta and Walter Payton set up Thomas's winning three-pointer.

SOURCE: Voting of the 29 members of the Pro Football Hall of Fame, 25 of whom returned ballots.

Woody Hayes' 5 Greatest Explosions

1. December 29, 1978—Hitting Clemson's Charlie Bauman after the linebacker had intercepted an Art Schlichter pass that ended a Buckeye drive in the closing seconds of the game and sealed a 17-15 Gator Bowl victory for Clemson.

2. November 20, 1971—Breaking two sideline markers over his knee in front of a national television audience in protest of an official's call. It made every major newscast that night and was pictured on every major sports page.

3. November 19, 1977—Shoving a mini-cam, hand-held camera, into the face of ABC-TV photographer Mike Freedman, who was trying to get a close-up of Hayes after the Buckeyes had lost the ball and the football game to Michigan. A national television audience viewed this and Hayes received a one-year probationary penalty from Big Ten Commissioner Wayne Duke.

4. December 29, 1978—Pounding on Ohio State junior guard Ken Fritz as Fritz tried to hold back Hayes after Hayes had attacked Clemson's Bauman (above). That picture made the wires and all major sports pages and national television. Hayes was fired after the game.

5. December 28, 1973—Shoving a camera into the face of a photographer who was taking pre-Rose Bowl publicity pictures at Pasadena, Calif.

Submitted by Sandy Schwartz, Executive Sports Editor, Columbus *Citizen-Journal*.

Dave Newhouse's 10 Greatest Rose Bowl Feats

Dave Newhouse, veteran journalist on the Oakland *Tribune*, coauthored *Rose Bowl Football Since 1902* with Herb Michelson.

1. Roy Riegels' wrong-way run in 1929 (misdirected, but a feat nonetheless).
2. UCLA's 14-12 shocker over mighty Michigan State in 1966.
3. Fourth-stringer Doyle Nave's touchdown pass that gave USC a 7-3 victory over unbeaten, untied, unscored-upon Duke in 1939.
4. Columbia's 7-0 upset of Stanford's Vow Boys in 1934.
5. Stanford's 27-17 defeat of Woody Hayes' best Ohio State team in 1971.
6. Little Washington and Jefferson holding California's Wonder Team to a scoreless tie in 1922.
7. Ron VanderKelen's passing performance (he completed 33 of 48 passes) for Wisconsin against USC in 1963 in a losing cause. USC won, 42-37.
8. USC's 18-17 comeback victory over Ohio State in 1975.
9. Oregon State's stunning 20-16 victory over Duke in the only Rose Bowl game not played in Pasadena; 1942 in Durham, N.C.
10. USC's Charles White scoring a touchdown without the football to beat Michigan, 14-7, in 1979.

USC's Pat Haden threw for the final touchdown and passed for the two-point conversion that beat Ohio State, 18-17, in 1975.

USC/Sports Photo Source

John Gagliardi's 12 Outrageous Rules for Coaching Football

John Gagliardi is the unique and rather unorthodox head football coach at St. John's (Minn.) University who abides by the following rules:

1. No scrimmaging at any time
2. No blocking sleds
3. No tackling dummies
4. No tackling in practice
5. No playbooks
6. No squad meetings after college classes begin
7. No play-calling from the bench
8. No assistant in the press box with headphones to the sidelines
9. No athletic scholarships
10. No grading of football players by game films
11. No weight training
12. No running after practice

SOURCE: Cincinnati *Post.*

Harold Rosenthal's 10 Most-Memorable Football Quotes

"Football," said Vince Lombardi, "is a game of blocking and tackling played down in the dirt." He should have added that a lot of conversation also goes on before, during, and after the game. Here are the 10 most memorable quotes Harold Rosenthal, veteran football observer, writer, and publicist, has heard from goalpost to goalpost.

1. "Win one for the Gipper."—This is attributed to George Gipp, famed Notre Dame back who died while still a player. It's a piece of his death-bed bequest to Knute Rockne; asking Rockne to tell his teams, when the going got rough, to "go out and win one for the Gipper." The part of George Gipp in the movie *Knute Rockne—All-American* was played by Ronald Reagan. Pat O'Brien was Knute Rockne.
2. "We'll not only win the Super Bowl, I'll guarantee it." —This was Joe Namath, New York Jets quarterback, a couple of evenings prior to the Super Bowl III upset victory over the Baltimore Colts after the Jets were rated 17-point underdogs. Namath made this statement, tall glass in hand, at a Touchdown Club dinner in Miami.

Pat O'Brien, right, with Amos Alonzo Stagg, played the lead role in *Knute Rockne—All-American.*

UPI

Had the Jets lost, the quote would have been dead for more than a decade.

3. "Two out of three ain't bad."—This was Tex Schramm's reaction to a personal attack by Dallas running back Duane Thomas, in which he called the president of the Cowboys "a liar, a thief and a crook." Thomas also called Cowboy coach Tom Landry "a plastic man."
4. "The mind can absorb only what the seat can endure." —Allie Sherman's evaluation of the learning process in football blackboard work when, as coach of the New York Giants, he watched defensive tackles sleep with their eyes open.
5. "If you cheat, your wives will be the first to know because I'll tell them."—Paul Brown's annual dictum upon opening training camp with the Cleveland Browns

Michigan center Gerald Ford — "without his helmet."

Michigan/Sports Photo Source

and later the Cincinnati Bengals. Brown ran a tight ship and felt that concentrating on beating the Pittsburgh Steelers provided all the intellectual entertainment his troops needed.

6. "There hasn't been anything new in football in the last 50 years."—This was Red Grange's commentary on how far football had come since the days he was the "Galloping Ghost," No. 77, in the late 1920s. Obviously, according to Grange, not very far.
7. "The older we get, the faster we ran as a boy."—Steven Owen's tribute to the adaptability of the human mind and its ability to retain only the more pleasant memories. Owen was a prime example of the "Faster we ran, etc." philosophy. Head coach of the New York Giants for 22 years, he wound up close to the 300-pound mark, so it was obvious he had run faster as a boy.
8. "It looked like a Chinese fire drill."—This was Hank Stram's evaluation of the Minnesota Vikings' futile attempts to defense the Kansas City Chiefs' formidable attack in Super Bowl IV. So what happens? Bud Grant, the Vikings' head coach in that game, is still coaching and Stram is long since gone to TV wonderland.
9. "Nothing you will ever do the rest of your lives will be as important."—Howard Jones' admonition to the Yale football players on the eve of the annual game with Harvard, back in 1913. Jones was Yale's first paid football coach.
10. "He played too many times without his helmet."—Lyndon Johnson's scornful evaluation of Gerald Ford when the former Michigan center was minority leader in Congress.

Putt Powell's All-Time University of Oklahoma Football Team Made Up of Players from Texas

The intense rivalry between the universities of Texas and Oklahoma in football extends beyond the gridiron to the recruiting battlefield. It is a coup for Texas to recruit players from Oklahoma and for Oklahoma to recruit players from Texas. Putt Powell of the Amarillo (Tex.) *Globe-News* has covered the last 41 Texas-Oklahoma games and has seen all of these Texans star for Oklahoma.

OFFENSE

Ends—Dub Wooten, Amarillo, 1943; Billy Brooks, Austin, 1975.
Tackles—Eddie Foster, Monahans, 1973; Bob Harrison, Stamford, 1958.
Guards—Greg Roberts, Nacogdoches, 1978; Billy White, Amarillo, 1961.
Center—Jerry Tubbs, Breckenridge, 1956.
Quarterback—Jack Mildren, Abilene, 1971.
Running backs—Billy Sims, Hooks, 1978; Joe Washington, Port Arthur, 1975: Greg Pruitt, Houston, 1972.
Place-kicker—Uwe von Schamann, Fort Worth, 1978.

DEFENSE

Ends—George Cumby, Gorman, 1977; Tom Brahaney, Midland, 1972.
Tackles—Jim Weatherall, White Deer, 1951; Ed Gray, Odessa, 1956.
Guard—J. D. Roberts, Dallas, 1953.
Linebackers—Myrle Greathouse, Amarillo, 1948; Daryl Hunt, Odessa, 1978; Carl McAdams, White Deer, 1965.
Backs—Monty Johnson, Amarillo, 1970; Zac Henderson, Burkburnett, 1977; Scott Hill, Hurst, 1976.
Punter—Joe Wylie, Henderson, 1971.

Leonard Koppett's Checklist of 15 Pieces of Information That Are Useful, Customary, and Practical for the Highly Interested, But Not Obsessed, Follower of Professional Football for Full Appreciation of the Game

1. The names and numbers of the players.
2. Something about the general characteristics of the most

prominent players: which runner's asset is speed, strength, or shiftiness; which receiver is a great catcher or exceptionally fast, or both; which defensive lineman is noted for his pass-rush ability; what the punter can ordinarily do and how accurate the field goal kicker is.

3. The name and, to a degree, the personality of the head coach, and perhaps some of the assistants on his staff.
4. Something about the general approach to football of this coach: pass-oriented, run-oriented, defense-oriented, gung-ho, calm-and-organized, inspirational-paranoid, conservative, innovative, or whatever.
5. The recent record and history of the team.
6. The names and characteristics of a few key players on each week's opposing team.
7. The general style of play that you can expect from this week's opponent.
8. The won-lost standings of the league, and the immediate possibilities.
9. Some general principles of football strategy: that you don't try for first-down yardage on fourth down in your own territory, that second-and-long is a more likely passing situation than third-and-short, how time is saved in the last two minutes, and basic stuff of that sort.
10. A working knowledge of the playing rules (like the fact that an NFL receiver must have both feet in bounds while a college pass can be completed with only one foot in).
11. Various offensive formations used by your team and what they imply by the play coming up.
12. Different defensive alignments, and what they "give" to the offense (in a very general way).
13. Special tasks of certain players, such as a fifth defensive back who comes in on obvious passing downs.
14. The implications of a second tight end or a third wide receiver on a particular play.
15. The standard score-down-yardage choices your team usually makes.

Doug Huff's 7 Most Productive Backs, 6 Most Productive Teams, and 4 Most Outstanding Kicking Efforts in High School Football

Doug Huff, sports editor of the Wheeling (W.Va.) *Intelligencer*, is also contributing editor to the first-ever *National High School Sports Record Book* published by the National Federation of State High School Associations and author of the annual national prep record review for Street & Smith's *Basketball Yearbook*.

BACKS

1. Ken Hall, Sugar Land (Texas) High, 1950-53—He rushed for 11,232 yards including 4,045 in 12 games his senior year which was highlighted by an 11-carry, 520-yard game; he scored 899 points on 127 touchdowns and 137 conversions, including 395 points (57 TDs, 53 PATs) his senior season. Hall's career total offense standard is 14,558 yards.
2. Ron Cuccia, Wilson High, Los Angeles, 1975-77—This "Italian Stallion" run-and-pass quarterback chalked up 11,451 total offense yards and accounted for 145 TDs in 38 games while playing for father-coach; he completed 528 of 869 passes for 8,804 yards and 91 TDs including 66 TDs and 6,414 yards his last two seasons. In one game as a sophomore, he completed 31 of 41 passes for 513 yards in a 571-yard total offense effort; in another, he completed 34 of 39 aerials for 509 yards and seven TDs in a half.
3. Sal Gonzales, Gadsden High, Anthony (N.M.), 1952-55—This single-wing tailback handled the ball on about every play of 38 games and surpassed the 9,000-yard and 600-point totals for his four-year tenure.
4. Billy Simms, Hooks (Texas) High, 1972-74—One of the most productive prep phenoms, he made the biggest splash later on with a Heisman Trophy at the U. of Oklahoma and was a rookie sensation with the Detroit Lions; he

amassed 7,738 career rushing yards, including 3,080 as a junior.

5. Steve Tate, Luther (Okla.) High, 1973-76—He rushed for 7,656 yards including 3,383 as a junior.
6. David Overstreet, Big Sandy (Texas) High, 1973-76—Later a running mate of Sims at the U. of Oklahoma, he was the main cog in Big Sandy's 1975 team which scored 820 points in 14 games and he rushed for 3,032 yards; his career figure was 7,652.
7. Pat Haden, Bishop Amat High, LaPuente (Calif.), 1968-70—He later starred at USC and played for the Los Angeles Rams, but raised eyebrows as a schoolboy with 7,633 passing yards including 6,291 his final two seasons; he connected on 527 of 850 career aerials and 82 TDs, including 207 for 3,383 yards and 48 TDs (29 one season) to favorite receiver, J. K. McKay, Jr., son of the Tampa Bay Buccaneer coach.

TEAMS

1. Jersey Shore (Pa.) High, 1922—This "adding machine" offense racked up 676 points in nine games for a 75.1 per game average.
2. Fostoria (Ohio) High, 1912—Scoreboard operators were busy for eight games with 596 points and a 74.5 per game gait.
3. Haven (Kansas) High, 1927—This offensive-minded squad boosted its 72.4-point per game average (578 in eight games) with an all-time record 256-0 lacing of Sylvia High, featuring 38 TDs and 28 conversions including 90 points and 13 TDs by Elvin McCoy. No opponents crossed the Haven goal line all season.
4. Hugo (Colo.) High, 1930—This squad amassed 748 points in 11 starts for a 68.0 average.
5. Steele High, Dayton, Ohio, 1920—This team scored 600 points in nine outings for a 66.7 norm.
6. Harrisburg (Pa.) Tech, 1918—They allowed 10 points to nine opponents while scoring 597 for a 66.3 average. The next season, Tech averaged "only" 58.4 (701 points in 12 starts), but recorded 12 shutouts.

KICKING

1. Kim Braswell, Avondale (Ga.) High, 1965-68—He never missed in 134 conversion attempts during his prep career before setting kicking standards at the University of Georgia.
2. Bruno Konopka, Manual High, Denver (Colo.), 1937—In a game against city rival Denver South, he boomed a punt 77 yards in the air. The ball kept rolling until it came to rest 132 yards, six inches away, according to a measurement. South, however, won the game, 7-6, as Konopka missed on a drop-kick conversion attempt.
3. Russell Wheatley, Permian High, Odessa (Texas), 1975—In a state playoff semifinal game at Lubbock, this five-foot, seven-inch, 150-pounder placekicked a 62-yard field goal in the final minutes to give his team a 10-9 victory.
4. Kelly Imhoff, Kent (Wash.) High, 1929—He matched Wheatley's longest effort 46 years earlier against Arlington High—with a drop kick.

Curt Gowdy's 18 Tips for Young Football Players

1. In blocking or tackling, always keep your head up.
2. Don't leave your feet when blocking or tackling. Get as close to your opponents as possible before making your move.
3. After making contact on a block, keep your legs spread and keep them moving with short, digging steps.
4. Tackle with your shoulder. Drive it hard into the ball-carrier, pull him toward you and fall on top of him.
5. When passing, throw overhand off a firmly planted back foot. Step directly toward your target with the other foot and follow through with your arm.
6. Catch a pass with your hands, then pull it into your body. Catch balls below waist with fingers down, those above waist with fingers up.
7. In punting, depress your toes and snap your lower leg into the ball. Keep the other foot on the ground—don't jump.

8. In place-kicking, meet the ball about one-third of the way up the seam and keep your head down from start to finish.
9. In ball-carrying, keep your legs comfortably apart and lift your knees. Keep your hand over the near end of the ball, with the other end of the ball secured near your armpit. Carry the ball under the arm farthest from the closest tacklers.
10. As quarterback, make your handoffs from belt buckle to belt buckle.
11. Centers: after passing the ball, lift your head instantly and move forward.
12. In pulling out of the line, stay low and keep driving your arms.
13. Defensive backs: never let an opponent get behind you. Always think of the pass first and the run second. Watch your man, not the ball, until the pass is thrown.
14. Defensive ends: try to turn every play to the inside.
15. Defensive linemen: whenever the ball-carrier takes off in the opposite direction, pursue him. If he is delayed anywhere along the line, you will often be able to catch up to him.
16. Run hard and hit hard. It's the player who takes it easy who is often injured.
17. Wear the best equipment you can afford; the better the equipment, the longer it lasts and the better it protects you.
18. When practicing in very hot weather, wear light equipment, get a supply of salt tablets, and never work out for too long.

SOURCE: *The Family Pro Football TV Handbook.*

V

The Mating Game

Morganna's "10 Favorite Baseball Players I Would Most Like To Run Out on the Field and Kiss"

Exotic dancer (with an emphasis on the former) Morganna is known as "Baseball's Kissing Bandit," a name she picked up because of her little (?) habit of leaving her seat and running onto the field to kiss ballplayers. She does it wearing sneakers, shorts, and a sweater; a very, VERY tight sweater.

She started this act in 1969, when she busted onto the field of play to smooch Pete Rose. In more than 10 years of kissing, Morganna has managed to get onto the field 12 times and scored on all but two occasions.

"A pretty good batting average, huh!" she points out.

She has no intention of retiring and plans to continue dashing onto the field when the mood strikes her. She nailed George Brett at the 1980 All-Star Game and he went to the top of her list.

1. George Brett—He's a great kisser and a fantastic baseball player.
2. Jim Palmer—He looks so cute in his undies.
3. Rick Cerone—I'm from the South and my grandmother told me never to kiss a Yankee, but for him I'll make an exception.

Morganna makes contact with George Brett at the 1977 All-Star Game in Seattle's Kingdome.
UPI

The other view.
Sports Photo Source

4. Pete Rose—He's always been my baseball idol.
5. Steve Carlton—I've always liked the strong, silent type.
6. Nolan Ryan
7. Tom Seaver
8. Fred Lynn
9. Bucky Dent
10. (tie) Joe Garagiola—My favorite baseball announcer.
    San Diego Chicken—My favorite chicken.
    Billy Martin—My favorite manager.

George McGann's 10 Tennis Love Matches

George McGann, who has been eyeing the world tennis scene from a press box for more years than he cares to remember, has observed the following Love Matches:

1. Harry and Nell Hopman—Harry is the famed Australian Davis Cup captain, team disciplinarian deluxe, and coach. Nell was a top player as well as official and manager of touring Australian women's teams.
2. Harry and Lucy Hopman—After Nell's death, Harry married American Lucy Fox, who shares his new life as a tennis camp director in Florida.
3. Charles and Mary Hare—This British couple, both international players, for many years have lived in Chicago where Charlie works for Wilson Sporting Goods.
4. John and Chris Evert Lloyd—Chris Evert was the first of the American teenage two-handed backhander marvels and her marriage to English touring pro John Lloyd was a major event. Both continued their tennis careers.
5. Roger and Evonne Cawley—Evonne Goolagong, the graceful Australian, resumed her career after marriage to Englishman Roger Cawley and birth of daughter Kelly Alana.
6. Jimmy and Patti Connors—Volatile Jimmy claimed marriage to the former Playboy centerfolder, and subsequent fatherhood, calmed him down and improved his tennis.
7. Lew and Jenny Hoad—These attractive Australians have raised a family in Spain, where they both run a tennis hotel. They married at Wimbledon in the early fifties when they were members of the touring Australian teams.
8. Stan and Marjory Smith—Stan, all-time great doubles star, and Marjory Gengler, a fine player herself, have lent dignity and charm to the game.
9. Bill and Nancy Talbert—Bill has had one of the outstanding careers in tennis—as player, Davis Cup captain and tournament director of the U.S. Open. At his side is the lovely Nancy Pike, outstanding hostess and mother

Chris Evert Lloyd and husband John played a charity match against Bjorn Borg and Mariana Simionescu (now Mrs. Borg) in the spring of 1980.

UPI

of two sons.

10. Bobby Riggs and himself—No comment. But if necessary, Bobby will provide all the comment you could possibly want.

Bob Paul's 12 Greatest Olympic Romances

Bob Paul is Director of Communications for the United States Olympic Committee.

1. In 1920, the first Olympic team shipboard-romance, Alice Lord, diving, and Richmond Landon, 1920 high jump champion. The marriage lasted a long time before Dick succumbed after a long illness.
2. In 1968, at Mexico City, Vera Caslavska, all-around gold in gymnastics in 1964 and 1968, wed middle distance runner Josef Odlozil, also from Czechoslovakia, in an impressive service at the Olympic village.
3. Russian figure skater Irina Rovnina, after winning in 1972, got herself a new partner, Alexandr Zaitsev. They won again in 1980.
4. First big one in pairs skating was Andree Joly and Pierre Brunet of France, 1928 champions. They repeated at Lake Placid in 1932, are still active in figure skating and have deserted their native land for the United States.
5. Best for the United States in pairs skating are Carol Heiss (1960 singles champion) and Hayes Alan Jenkins (1956 singles champion). They are still happily married and both do a great deal to promote the United States Olympic Committee.
6. The most publicized marriage brought together Olga Fikotova, Czechoslovakia, 1956 discus champion, and Harold Connolly, United States, 1956 hammer throw champion. Olga became an American citizen and competed with Harold on the 1960 team and by herself in 1964 and 1968 before calling it quits—both track and the marriage.
7. A romance growing out of the 1976 Olympic Games was hurdler Patrice Donnelly and shot-

Two Olympic champions, Olga Fikotova of Czechoslovakia and Harold Connolly of the United States, were married in Prague in 1957.

UPI

putter Peter Schmock. Patrice retired, but Peter won the 1980 Olympic trials.

8. Muriel Davis, 16, was a member of the United States gymnastics team, as was Abie Grossfeld, 22, at Melbourne in 1956. They were married within a year. The union lasted for more than 15 years and although the marriage ended in divorce, it is still a great Olympic romance.
9. From 1976, we have the idyllic romance bringing together Roland Matthes, 1968 and 1972 Olympic backstroke champion, and Kornelia Ender, who won a flock of medals for East Germany in 1976 at Montreal. They have at least one child and the world awaits the offspring's first venture into the competitive pool.
10. Perhaps this is not an Olympic romance, but Emil Zatopek, winner of the 5,000 and 10,000 meter runs and the marathon in 1952, was the

husband of the 1952 javelin throw gold medalist, Dana Zatopekova.

11. My favorite Olympic romance resulted in the marriage of Bill Toomey, United States 1968 Olympic decathlon winner, and Mary Rand, Great Britain's long jump winner in 1964. They met at the third practice Olympic Games in Mexico in 1967. Mary was injured and could not compete in the 1968 Games, but was there as a commentator for the BBC and within 18 months they were wed.
12. Mary Mairs made her debut with the equestrian team at Rome in 1960 and met Frank Chapot, who had been on one previous team. Soon after, they were married. Chapot continued to ride with our jumpers in 1968 and 1972 and Mary retired from active riding after the 1968 Games.

Dianne Grosskopf's 5 Sexiest Athletes

1. Jim Palmer—"So different, physically, from the normal run of pitchers. He's got a body like a model, and he's not afraid to show it off."
2. Ted Turner—"Knows what he wants and goes after it, whether it be starting the Cable News Network or winning the America's Cup. Women admire this more than ever, now that they are tackling greater tasks themselves."
3. Pat Haden—"The fact that he was a Rhodes scholar shows that he is not only an athlete, but intelligent."
4. Harold Solomon—"Great style and composure. Unlike other tennis players I've seen, he never blames any of his own errors on others."
5. Lee Mazzilli—"Our readers love him."

Note: Ms. Grosskopf is executive editor of *Playgirl* Magazine. She compiled this list for *Inside Sports.*

Baltimore pitcher Jim Palmer sells Jockey brand underwear.
Jockey/Sports Photo Source

Seattle Mariners Wives' 10 Handsomest Major League Players

1. Jim Palmer
2. Rick Honeycutt
3. Jim Rice
4. Bucky Dent
5. George Brett
6. Joe Simpson
7. Paul Molitor
8. Bill Russell
9. Dwight Evans
10. Ken Singleton

SOURCE: Bellevue (Wash.) *Journal-American*.

Larry Bird's exciting passes produce baskets and expressions of awe from onlookers.

Wide World

VI

Slam Dunk

Steve Hershey's All-Time Basketball Ratings of Fans, Leapers, Non-Leapers, Passers, Non-Passers, Pure Shooters, Brick Shooters, Defenders, Floorburners, and Nicknames

Steve Hershey, captain of the shoot-from-the-hip team, covers the pros for the Washington *Star*.

FANS

Most Loyal—Milwaukee, where the Bucks have played before 91 percent capacity through all those long losing streaks, coaching changes, snowstorms, and other distractions in the past 10 years.

Least Loyal—Los Angeles, where the fans arrive fashionably late, usually sit with their arms folded as they would in nearby movie houses, and appear to have the smug attitude of "entertain me."

Most Appreciative—Portland, where every game is a sellout and the fans sit in almost cathedral-like silence, then wildly applaud after every good play.

Most Imaginative—The fans who sit in those awful seats high above Boston's parquet floor and drape such bedsheet signs as "Our Carr Runs on Green Gas" and "Maxwell is Good to the Last Drop."

Most Enthusiastic—Like kids with a new toy, the fans at the Salt Palace in Salt Lake City resemble a high school crowd as they cheer wildly at every move by the home team and never, never show any displeasure toward the tail-end Jazz.

Least Enthusiastic—Perhaps it's the serene surroundings, but it seems that the spectators at the Oakland Coliseum are just killing time before the night life starts across the bridge in San Francisco.

It hardly seems fair to select a mere five players to be honored as the best at their positions at the end of each NBA season. Comparing rebounders with scorers, ball-handlers with shooters, and substitutes with starters is to ignore the special talents that make the league so unpredictable. With this in mind, here are enough mythical teams to give all the specialists their proper recognition, whether they like it or not.

ALL-LEAPERS

Forwards—Julius Erving and Terry Tyler
Guards—David Thompson and Lloyd Free
Center—George Johnson

ALL-NON-LEAPERS

Forwards—Coby Dietrick and Kevin Restani
Guards—John Lucas and John Roche
Center—Wes Unseld

ALL-PASSERS

Forwards—John Johnson and Larry Bird
Guards—Magic Johnson and Phil Ford
Center—Clifford Ray

ALL-NON-PASSERS

Forwards—John Drew and Mike Mitchell
Guards—Lloyd Free and Brian Taylor
Center—Darryl Dawkins

ALL-PURE SHOOTERS

Forwards—Campy Russell and Scott Wedman
Guards—George Gervin and Otis Birdsong
Center—Kareem Abdul-Jabbar

ALL-BRICK SHOOTERS

Forwards—Gar Heard and Jim Brewer
Guards—Quinn Buckner and Lionel Hollins
Center—George Johnson

ALL-DEFENSIVE

Forwards—Caldwell Jones and Dan Roundfield
Guards—Dennis Johnson and Gus Williams
Center—Kareem Abdul-Jabbar

ALL-FLOORBURN

Forwards—Mitch Kupchak and Allen Bristow
Guards—Ron Lee and Mike Newlin
Center—(A pivot man hasn't hit the floor since Dave Cowens retired.)

ALL-NICKNAME

Forwards—Dr. J. and Truck
Guards—Magic and Tiny
Center—Tree

ALL-MATADOR DEFENSE

Forwards—Larry Kenon and John Drew
Guards—(Pick any two shooting guards)
Center—Kent Benson

George Gervin is the purest of the pure shooters.

San Antonio/Sports Photo Source

5 Nicknames of Professional Basketball Teams We'll Never (Thankfully) See Again

1. Berwick Carbuilders
2. Lebanon Seltzers
3. Trenton Pat Pavers
4. Cherry Hill Rookies
5. Hamden Bics (named for the ball-point pen)

Herm Rogul's 21 Well-Nicknamed Philadelphia Basketball Legends

As a Philadelphia sports historian, Herm Rogul, of the Philadelphia *Bulletin,* has a fascination for basketball and nicknames, the best of which he has listed here.

1. Lewis (Black Magic) Lloyd
2. Fran (White Magic) McCaffery
3. Linda (Hawkeye) Page
4. Frank (Watusi) Card
5. Anthony (Stinky) Norris
6. Gail (Pillsbury) Doughty
7. Tom (Trooper) Washington
8. Earl (Magic, Vernon, Jesus, The Pearl) Monroe
9. Sam (Wobbles) White
10. Darryl (City Lights) Warwick
11. Leroy (Sweets) Alexander
12. Fran (Rainbow Johnson) O'Hanlon
13. (Psychedelic) Eddie Mast
14. Fred (Mad Dog) Carter
15. Joe (Jellybean) Bryant
16. Bob (Sweeper) Stephens
17. Gene (Tinker Bell) Banks
18. Armando (Cheese) Burnette
19. George (Silver Quill) Kiseda
20. Kevin (Barney Google) Beaford
21. Greg (Box) Brandon

Ted St. Martin's Top 10 Free-Throw Shooters of All Time

Modestly, or maybe not so modestly, Ted St. Martin bills himself as the world's premier free-throw shooter. He makes a living traveling around the United States and accepting challenges in free-throw shooting, and the 45-year-old St. Martin has humiliated many a local hero. He holds the record for having made 2,036 consecutive free throws.

1. Ted St. Martin—I have to rate myself first because of the consecutive strings I have had and the fact that I take on all challengers by the thousands each year, including pros, college, and high school players all over the U.S. and Canada.

2. Bill Sharman—His record as a Celtic speaks for itself. Bill beat me once in a shoot-off of 100 shots, but he was also my idol and the awe of it all had some effect.

3. Rick Barry—It's hard to put a man who has the highest percentage in an NBA career in third place. Also I had the pleasure to shoot with him on "The Mike Douglas Show."

4. Fred Newman—This man would have to be near the top since he made over 98 percent in 24 hours of continuous shooting and many consecutive while blindfolded. I had the pleasure to shoot with Fred in 1974 and 1975. He didn't beat me, but then few have.

5. Bunny Leavitt—He made a string of 499 consecutive shots way back in the 1930s. If he was at his peak in this day, he might be the one to outdo me.

6. Hal Cohen—As a high school player, he once made 598 in a row.

7. Wilfred Hetzel—A trick shooter, but he could throw foul shots underhanded like a softball and make them.
8. Mack Calvin—Denver player who was one of the top shooters in the old ABA and who also beat me once in a

string of 100 shots.

9. Jerry Colangelo—Also a former great ABA shooter and now general manager of the Phoenix Suns. He beat me at a halftime performance, but I got my revenge and beat him the next year at another halftime performance.

10. (tie) Larry Kopczyk, Wayne Purvis, James Lister, Jr.—These had to be mentioned. Kopczyk was one of the best in the NCAA in the spring of 1980. Purvis, an Alabama high school coach, is a 95 percent shooter. Lister sustained an injury early in his career or he would have gone on to the top with his determination.

James D. Drucker's 4 Unusual Occupations of Owners of Minor League Basketball Teams

James D. Drucker is Commissioner of the Continental Basketball Association, the country's oldest pro basketball league.

1. Owner of the Board of Trade Saloon, Nome, Alaska—Jim West, Sr., owner of the Billings Volcanos. The Board of Trade was originally owned by Tex Rickard, who later went on to build the third Madison Square Garden.
2. President of a guitar manufacturing company—Frank Martin, president of Martin Guitars and great grandson of the company's founder, owner of the Lehigh Valley Jets. Martin Guitars has been building guitars since 1850.
3. Proctologist—Dr. Seymour Kilstein, owner of the Philadelphia Kings. He operates where it really counts.
4. Underwater demolition expert—Roger Jacobson of Anchorage, Alaska, owner of the Anchorage Northern Knights. Jacobson made his fortune as an underwater demolition expert. His talents were invaluable for the underwater exploration of oil when the Alaskan pipeline was built.

The Opening Day Roster of the Cleveland Cavaliers Who Set a Standard for Futility in 1970-71 with a Record of 15-67 in Their First Season in the NBA

NO.	PLAYER	COLLEGE
5.	Bobby Lewis	North Carolina
7.	Bobby Smith	Tulsa
10.	Joel Cooke	Indiana
11.	John Warren	St. John's
15.	Dave Sorenson	Ohio State
18.	McCoy McLemore	Drake
21.	Johnny Egan	Providence
22.	Cliff Anderson	St. Joseph's
32.	John Johnson	Iowa
40.	Gary Suiter	Midwestern (Tex.)
44.	Walt Wesley	Kansas
45.	Luther Rackley	Xavier (Ohio)
50.	Len Chappell	Wake Forest

Submitted by Joe Tait, Cavaliers' play-by-play announcer since their first season.

12 Pro Basketball Players Who Have Played on NBA Championship Teams for Two Different Franchises

1. Arnie Risen—Rochester (1950-51) and Boston (1956-57)
2. Slater Martin—Minneapolis (1949-50, 1951-52, 1952-53, 1953-54) and St. Louis (1957-58).
3. Walter (Buddy) Davis—Philadelphia (1955-56) and St. Louis (1957-58)
4. Jack Coleman—Rochester (1950-51) and St. Louis (1957-58)
5. Clyde Lovellette—Minneapolis (1953-54) and Boston (1962-63, 1963-64)
6. Wilt Chamberlain—Philadelphia (1966-67) and Los Angeles (1971-72)

Wilt Chamberlain won his second NBA championship as a Los Angeles Laker in 1972.

UPI

7. Charles Johnson—Golden State (1974-75) and Washington (1977-78)
8. Bobby Dandridge—Milwaukee (1970-71) and Washington (1977-78)
9. Paul Silas—Boston (1973-74, 1975-76) and Seattle (1978-79)
10. Wally Walker—Portland (1976-77) and Seattle (1978-79)
11. Kareem Abdul-Jabbar—Milwaukee (1970-71) and Los Angeles (1979-80)
12. Jamaal Wilkes—Golden State (1974-75) and Los Angeles (1979-80)

10 Winningest Active Major College Basketball Coaches (Through 1980)

COACH	VICTORIES
1. Ray Meyer, DePaul	623
2. Marv Harshman, Washington	547
3. Norm Sloan, Florida	477
4. Ralph Miller, Oregon State	471
5. Ned Wulk, Arizona State	458
6. Guy Lewis, Houston	453
7. Abe Lemons, Texas	443
8. Tex Winter, Long Beach State	414
9. Dean Smith, North Carolina	407
10. Lefty Driesell, Maryland	399

SOURCE: NCAA Statistics Service.

10 Winningest Active Division II Basketball Coaches (Through 1980)

COACH	VICTORIES
1. Clarence Gaines, Winston-Salem	658
2. Dom Rosselli, Youngstown State	570

3.	James Phelan, Mount St. Mary's	464
4.	Bobby Vaughn, Elizabeth City	413
5.	Bill Detrick, Central Connecticut	341
6.	Burt Kahn, Quinnipiac	337
7.	Jim Wink, Ferris State	334
8.	Dick DeHart, Millersville State	323
9.	Lucias Mitchell, Norfolk State	306
10.	Billy Key, Missouri-Rolla	298

SOURCE: NCAA Statistics Service.

10 Winningest Division III Basketball Coaches (Through 1980)

	COACH	VICTORIES
1.	Tom Feely, St. Thomas	417
2.	Wilbur Renken, Albright	413
3.	Dick Sauers, Albany (N.Y.) State	407
4.	Jerry Johnson, LeMoyne-Owen	371
5.	Mark Peterman, Tri-State	360
6.	Don Smith, Elizabethtown	313
7.	Ollie Gelston, Montclair State	311
8.	Ray Steffan, Kalamazoo	291
9.	Allen Svennington, Alaska-Fairbanks	289
10.	Bill Knapton, Beloit	289

SOURCE: NCAA Statistics Service.

37 Winningest Major College Basketball Coaches of All Time (Through 1980)

	COACH	VICTORIES
1.	Adolph Rupp	874
2.	Phog Allen	771
3.	Henry Iba	767
4.	Ed Diddle	759
5.	John Wooden	667
6.	Ray Meyer	623

A young coach then, Ray Meyer is with George Mikan, who on this night in 1945 scored 53 points for DePaul against Rhode Island.

UPI

7.	Cam Anderson	611
8.	Amory (Slats) Gill	599
9.	Paul (Tony) Hinkle	560
10.	Frank McGuire	550
11.	Marv Harshman	547
12.	Fred Enke	525
13.	Hec Edmondson	505
14.	Harold Anderson	504
15.	Jack Friel	496

16.	Ev Shelton	494
17.	Jack Gardner	486
18.	Norm Sloan	477
19.	Ralph Miller	471
20.	John (Taps) Gallagher	465
21.	Bill Reinhart	464
22.	Clarence (Nibs) Price	463
23.	Ned Wulk	458
24.	Guy Lewis	453
25.	Branch McCracken	451
26.	Peck Hickman	443
27.	Abe Lemons	443
28.	Eddie Hickey	435
29.	Nat Holman	423
30.	Ozzie Cowles	421
31.	Alex Severence	419
32.	Clair Bee	410
33.	Howard Cann	409
34.	Dean Smith	407
35.	Al McGuire	405
36.	Frank Keaney	403
37.	Howard Hobson	400

SOURCE: NCAA Statistics Service.

Jay Simon's 11 Greatest Basketball Players Never To Play in the NCAA Tournament

Since the NCAA basketball championship began in 1939, some 8,000 players have participated in what has become one of America's most closely followed sports events. Jay Simon began covering the tournament in 1940 and covered the finals and one of the regionals almost every year through 1966 when he escaped the newspaper business. Since then he's closely followed the tournament, first as sports information director at Kansas U., and more recently as just a fan and managing editor of *Golf Digest*.

1. Vince Boryla, Notre Dame (1945-46), Denver (1949)
2. Ed Macauley, St. Louis (1946-47-48-49)

3. Dick Groat, Duke (1950-51-52)
4. Walter Dukes, Seton Hall (1951-52-53)
5. Sihugo Green, Duquesne (1954-55-56)
6. Bailey Howell, Mississippi State (1957-58-59)
7. Walt Bellamy, Indiana (1959-60-61)
8. Terry Dischinger, Purdue (1960-61-62)
9. Rick Barry, Miami (1963-64-65)
10. Pete Maravich, Louisiana State (1968-69-70)
11. Julius Erving, Massachusetts (1969-70-71)

Socks askew as usual, Pete Maravich was a sight to behold in his heyday as a collegian at LSU.

Malcolm Emmons

VII

Of Skis and Skates and Ice Cream Cones

John Halligan's 7 Famous Hockey Fans

John Halligan, director of public relations and business manager of the New York Rangers, prints lists, oddities, and other nonsense in "Skimming the Surface," a column that appears in the Ranger program.

1. Tiny Tim—He loved hockey even before Miss Vickie.
2. Charles Schultz—On ice with Charlie Brown, Snoopy, and Woodstock.
3. Tony Bennett—A regular in the old Madison Square Garden.
4. John Mitchell—Played college hockey at Fordham.
5. Monty Hall—"Let's Make a Deal" and a former hockey broadcaster.
6. Yogi Berra
7. Steve Allen

John Halligan's 5 Improbable Hockey Players' Birthplaces

1. Zranjanin, Yugoslavia—Ivan Boldirev
2. Emsdetten, Germany—Walt Tkaczuk

3. Caracas, Venezuela—Rick Chartraw
4. Paraguay, South America—Willi Plett
5. Big Springs, Texas—Mike Christie

Favorite Actors and Actresses of 15 NHL Players

1. Lee Fogolin—Robert DeNiro and Jane Fonda
2. Richard Martin—James Coburn, Robert Redford, and Barbara Carrera
3. Robbie Ftorek—Lee Marvin and Julie Andrews
4. Gordie Roberts—Jon Voight and Jane Fonda
5. Al MacAdam—Charles Bronson and Barbra Streisand
6. Wayne Babych—Peter Sellers and Ann-Margret
7. Bengt-Ake Gustaffson—Clint Eastwood
8. Guy Charron—Clint Eastwood and Barbra Streisand
9. Jim Bedard—Jack Nicholson, Dan Akroyd, and Jane Fonda
10. Dennis Maruk—Charles Bronson and Jacqueline Bisset
11. Garry Unger—James Garner, Burt Reynolds and Faye Dunaway
12. Ron Grahame—John Wayne and Katharine Hepburn
13. Charles Simmer—John Wayne and Jill Clayburgh
14. Ted Bulley—Steve McQueen and Jane Fonda
15. Mark Howe—Charles Bronson and Bette Davis

SOURCE: *Goal* Magazine.

Favorite All-Time Movies of 12 NHL Players

1. Peter Sullivan—*Gentleman Jim*
2. Ron Chipperfield—*The Deer Hunter*
3. Bengt-Ake Gustaffson—*The Good, the Bad and the Ugly*
4. Guy Charron—*The Dirty Dozen*
5. Dennis Maruk—*A Shot in the Dark*
6. Jim Bedard—*The Wizard of Oz*
7. Bob Gainey—*M * A * S * H*
8. Jim Schoenfeld—*Rocky II*
9. Bernie Federko—*Young Frankenstein*

10. Jordy Douglas—*Jaws*
11. Bobby Smith—*Serpico*
12. Dave Farrish—*Rocky, Midnight Express,* most Clint Eastwood movies

SOURCE: *Goal* Magazine.

Bobby Orr's 6 Hardest Checkers

1. Johnny Bucyk—"He won the Lady Byng Trophy, indicative of good sportsmanship, but he was one of the cleanest and hardest open-ice hitters I ever saw."
2. Leo Boivin—"He could really deliver a good, clean, hip check."
3. Don Marcotte—"Boy, could he hit! I'd come out of practice with my teeth aching."
4. Tim Horton—"A very tough, clean hitter."
5. Derek Sanderson
6. Eddie Westfall

SOURCE: *Inside Sports.*

Derek Sanderson got high checkmarks from teammate Bobby Orr.

UPI

Persons with Whom 6 NHL Players Would Most Like To Be Marooned on a Deserted Island

1. Pat Price—One of my old coaches; I'd kill him.
2. Dave Tallon—Ursula Andress
4. Steve Payne—Candy Loving. Anyone who reads *Playboy* will agree, I'm sure.
4. Curt Bennett—Racquel Welch. I love her mind and also the physical structure that so aesthetically encloses it.
5. Jim Bedard—Any seven-foot blonde.
6. Brian Sutter—Naturally my wife Judy. What else am I supposed to say?

SOURCE: *Goal* Magazine.

Superstitions of 18 NHL Players

1. Ron Grahame—Stand on the blue line for the National Anthem, not in the goal crease. Have a black cat cross my path.
2. Charlie Simmer—Dress from right to left.
3. Ted Bulley—Put right shin pad on first and put tape on stick.
4. Mark Howe—All sorts.
5. Robert Picard—Put on all my left pieces of equipment first.
6. Ryan Walter—Put left skate on before right one.
7. Brian Engblom—I always put my equipment on in the same order and always tie up the right skate first.
8. Laurie Boschman—If things are going good for me, I will try to stick with the same routine.
9. Darcy Rota—If I spill salt, I throw it over my left shoulder.
10. Peter Sullivan—Don't cross sticks in dressing

room. Last one on the ice leaving the dressing room.

11. Guy Charron—The way I put on my uniform, always dress from left side first.
12. Dennis Maruk—Eating pre-game meals.
13. Bob Gainey—If a situation arises I may do the same thing today as I did yesterday if I had extremely good luck yesterday.
14. Bernie Federko—Before going on the ice, I always tie my right skate before my left. Always put my sweater on after everybody else does. And always leave the locker room last.
15. Jordy Douglas—Dress from right to left, wear the same clothes on good days, eat same food as day before if the day went well.
16. Bobby Smith—Get dressed identically before hockey games. Touch wood at mention of serious injury or accident.
17. Dave Farrish—I always put my hockey equipment on the same way every time, but this could be just a habit.
18. Jim Bedard—Not telling what my superstitions are.

SOURCE: *Goal* Magazine.

Clif Taylor's "10 Celebrities I Have Instructed on Shortee Skis"

Clif Taylor won the United States Ski Writers Association's Golden Quill award for "inventing the GLM Method of Teaching skiing, and thus aiding the nation's ski industry, ski areas and the American skiing public." A former college ski racer, he was a combat ski trooper in the Italian campaign in World War II, and the inventor of the Shortee Ski. He was elected to the Ski Hall of Fame in 1978 and has written three books: *Instant Skiing, Ski in a Day,* and *GLM—The New Way to Ski.*

Clif Taylor demonstrates the Shortee Ski
that he pioneered.

Sports Photo Source

1. Lowell Thomas
2. Art Linkletter
3. Laurance Rockefeller
4. Lorne Greene
5. David McCallum
6. Jim Lang
7. Tim Conway
8. Ann Miller
9. Commander Whitehead
10. Jack Paar

Stan Isaacs' 10 Best Chocolate Ice Creams

What, you ask, does this have to do with sports? Nothing, except that long-time Long Island *Newsday* sports columnist Stan Isaacs is a ratings freak. It's his favorite sport. Long before it became the fad to rate hamburgers, ketchups, and powerbrokers, Isaacs, who contributed to our first two volumes, was rating Street Corners in Brooklyn, Baroque Composers, Hockey Team uniforms, and the Seven Santini Brothers (the movers, not the wrestlers). Always, he keeps a tongue in cheek and is willing to amend these ratings at the drop of an angry letter.

But in one category, Isaacs has always been deadly serious—chocolate ice creams. "Isn't everybody?" he asks. Every year, Isaacs ferrets out chocolate ice cream recommendations near and far and conducts his own knock-down-drag-out tastings just before his annual ratings, the latest (his 18th annual) of which are listed here.

1. Haagen Dazs—the packaged is better than the hand-dipped.
2. Sedutto's, Staten Island, N.Y.
3. Bassett's, Philadelphia—not as good on the road as it is at the home base.
4. Trattoria, New York—very dark and heavy.
5. Breyer's, New York—the hand-dipped is better than the packaged though it is increasingly hard to come by.
6. Bud's, San Francisco
7. Rumpelmayer's, New York
8. Taggart's, Canton, Ohio—for some reason, I never get out to Canton and am relying here on the word of my

scouts, among them Lamar Hunt, the first to declare that "there is no ice cream worthy of greatness below the Mason-Dixon line."

9. Schrafft's, New York—the regular, not the Continental.
10. (tie) Nassau Ice Cream, Roslyn, N.Y.; The Brasserie, New York.

VIII

Indoor Fun and Games

Ira G. Corn, Jr.'s 10 Greatest Bridge Players, 10 Greatest Backgammon Players, and 15 Greatest Chess Players in the World Today

Ira G. Corn, Jr., is captain of The Aces, five times world champions since 1970; syndicated bridge columnist for United Features, and Chairman of the Board of the American Contract Bridge League. The games he plays extend to chess and backgammon, and in the industrial world he is Chairman of the Board of Michigan General Corporation. All of his lists are alphabetical.

BRIDGE

1. Giorgio Belladonna, Italy
2. Gabriel Chagas, Brazil
3. Paul Chemla, France
4. Benito Garozzo, Italy
5. Bob Hamman, United States
6. Sammy Kehela, Canada
7. Christopher Mari, France
8. Tim Seres, Australia
9. Paul Soloway, United States
10. Bob Wolff, United States

BACKGAMMON

1. Billy Eisenberg, Los Angeles
2. Tim Holland, New York City
3. Oswald Jacoby, Dallas
4. Montakkasis Kumar, Europe
5. Kyle Larson, San Francisco
6. Jason Lester, New York City
7. Roger Low, New York City
8. Paul McGriel, New York City
9. Chuck Papazian, San Francisco
10. Stan Tomchin, New York City

CHESS

1. Lev Alburt, United States
2. Roman Djindjihashvili, Israel
3. Florin Gheorghiu, Rumania
4. Robert Huebner, Germany
5. Anatoly Karpov, Russia
6. Gerry Kastarov, Russia
7. Victor Korchnoi, Switzerland
8. Bent Larsen, Denmark
9. Anthony Miles, England
10. Lev Polugavesky, Russia
11. Lajos Portisch, Hungary
12. Yasser Seirawan, United States
13. Boris Spassky, Russia
14. Mikhail Tal, Russia
15. Jan Timman, Holland

Notes Mr. Corn: "Nailing down the top chess players in the world today has proved to be a more difficult job than bridge or backgammon. I relied heavily on several chess experts. The only thing they have in common is they don't agree. Apparently there is a common and widespread judgment as to who the top players are and there is a very major reluctance to distinguish between those in the top 10 and those in the top 15 or 20. As a matter of fact, the list of the top 15 excludes two or three names which were frequently mentioned. One glaring absence is that of Bobby Fischer, who has not played a tournament in six years. The chess world places a great deal of importance on the current victories and current participation in major tournaments. Fischer's unwillingness to be involved has taken him off everybody's list."

Mrs. Edward J. Little's "10 Things I Can't Believe Sports Collectors Collect"

Mrs. Little of Toledo, Ohio, says her son, Jack, has been involved in some unusual trades and "has shown me ads in sports collecting publications. Some of them were unusual, to say the least. No doubt lots of people out there collect these items. It's just that I'm surprised they do at all."

1. Baseball card wrappers, $5 each. "And I threw these out by the hundreds."
2. Used ticket stubs—"Who wants someone else's ticket stubs?"
3. Whole tickets, unused—"Who wants these, the game's over?"
4. Sport schedules—"People pay money for these? The beer companies give them away."
5. Old scorecards, someone else's—"No matter how exciting the game, you didn't see it."
6. College basketball box scores—"My son sent basketball box scores to a collector who sent him baseball cards in exchange."
7. Peek football books—"The bank gave them away. They later sold for 75 cents each."
8. Error cards—"So there was a misprint, everybody makes mistakes."
9. Match book covers—"Without the matches, yet."
10. Display boxes—"Stores give these to the kids."

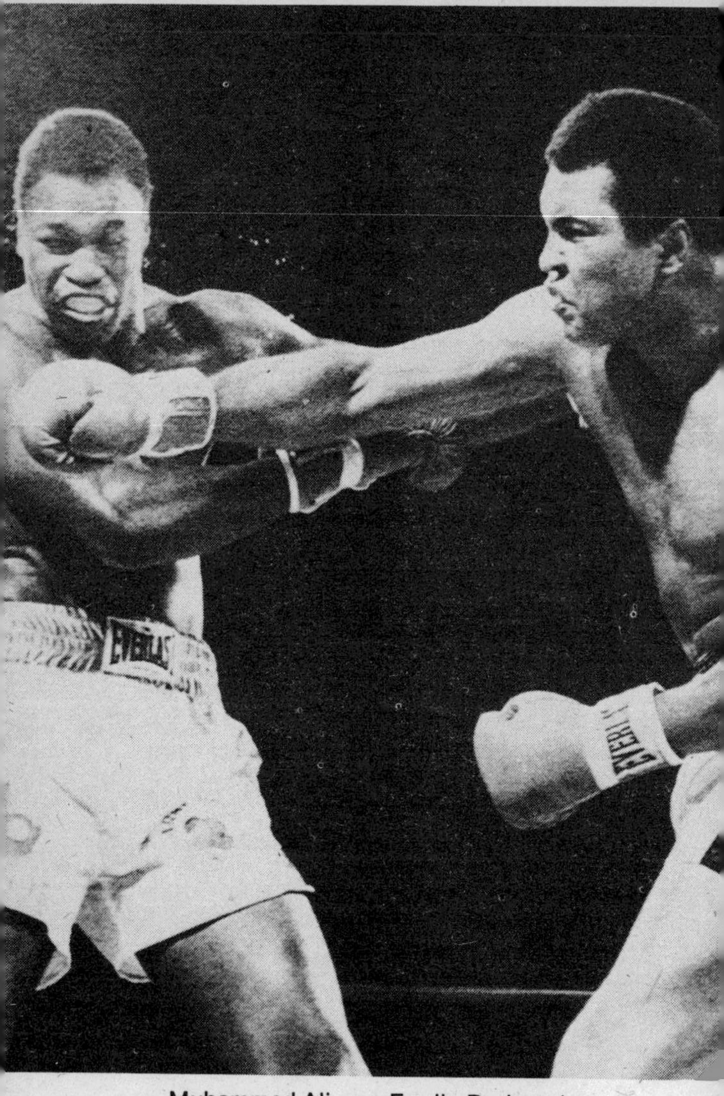

Muhammad Ali won Ferdie Pacheco's vote, but not for this performance in Las Vegas when Larry Holmes won their title bout on a TKO.

Wide World

IX

The Fighting Spirit

Dr. Ferdie Pacheco's 10 Greatest Boxers, 10 Greatest KO Artists, 10 Greatest Boxer-Punchers, 10 Questionable Fights, 6 Greatest Heavyweights, 10 Greatest Managers, 10 Best Non-Boxing Managers, 10 Best Cornermen, 10 Cornermen Braver Than Their Fighters

Medical doctor, artist, writer, cornerman, telecaster, Dr. Ferdie Pacheco was, for years, Muhammad Ali's personal physician and is currently Director of Boxing and on-air commentator for NBC. His credentials in boxing are outstanding and these lists, he says, "are prepared from a solely subjective point of view. They are limited to fighters, managers and assorted fight people that date from the '40s until the present. While I am in wonder and amazement at the legendary prowess of old fighters, I cannot honestly give my opinion since I did not personally see these great fight people in their prime."

GREATEST BOXERS

1. Muhammad Ali
2. Willie Pep
3. Sugar Ray Robinson
4. Luis Manuel Rodriguez
5. Joey Maxim
6. Sandy Saddler
7. Ezzard Charles
8. Harold Johnson
9. Tippy Larkin
10. Willie Pastrano

GREATEST KO ARTISTS

(One-punch destroyers)

1. Sonny Liston
2. Joe Louis
3. George Foreman
4. Rocky Marciano
5. Bob Satterfield
6. Roberto Duran
7. Wilfredo Gomez
8. Rocky Graziano
9. Florentino Fernandez
10. Cleveland Williams

GREATEST BOXER-PUNCHERS

(This exceptional category includes the men that embody the best of the science of boxing: they could dance and they could destroy.)

1. Roberto Duran
2. Carlos Monzon
3. Eder Jofre
4. Bob Foster
5. Kid Gavilan
6. Jose (Mantequilla) Napoles
7. Emile Griffith
8. Dick Tiger
9. Carlos Zarate
10. Marcel Cerdan

QUESTIONABLE FIGHTS

(Fights which had a strange smell about them.)

1. Muhammad Ali-Sonny Liston, second fight
2. Jersey Joe Walcott-Rocky Marciano, second fight
3. Chuck Davey-Chico Vejar
4. Jake LaMotta-Billy Fox
5. Joe Louis-Johnny Paycheck
6. Sonny Liston-Albert Westphal
7. Guadalupe Pintor-Carlos Zarate
8. Jose Napoles-Armando Muniz
9. Muhammad Ali-Sonny Liston, first fight
10. Jimmy Ellis-Floyd Patterson (Sweden)

GREATEST HEAVYWEIGHTS

(Includes only the past four decades; only six qualify as great.)

1. Muhammad Ali
2. Joe Louis
3. Rocky Marciano
4. Joe Frazier
5. Sonny Liston
6. George Foreman

GREATEST MANAGERS

(Men who can guide the ring fortunes, control the financial welfare, and, in every way, control the destiny of the fighter for his welfare.)

1. Angelo Dundee (Ali, Leonard, Ellis, Rodriguez)
2. Doc Kearns (Dempsey)
3. Cus D'Amato (Patterson)
4. Al Weill (Marciano)
5. Gil Clancy (Griffith)
6. Yancey (Yank) Durham (Frazier)
7. Lou Viscusi (Pep, Foster, Brown)
8. Jack McCoy (Palomino, Ramos)
9. Chris Dundee (Charles, Wolgast, Overlin)
10. Emanuel Steward (Hearns, Kenty)

BEST NON-BOXING MANAGERS

(Includes men not previously involved in boxing, who directed one fighter well and then dropped out of boxing when that fighter retired.)

MANAGER	PROFESSION	FIGHTER
1. Herbert Muhammad	Religion	Muhammad Ali
2. Mike Trainer	Lawyer	Sugar Ray Leonard
3. Bob Biron	Businessman	Ken Norton
4. Roy Cohn	Lawyer	Floyd Patterson
5. William Rosencrantz	Stockbroker	Ingemar Johansson
6. Ernesto Corral	Bus driver	Luis Rodriguez
7. Louisville Sponsor Group	Business	Cassius Clay
8. Peter Fuller	Politician	Tom McNeeley
9. E. Bennett Williams	Lawyer	Mike Baker
10. George Allen	Football coach	Mike Baker

BEST CORNERMEN

(Men who can inspire, outthink, direct, coach, teach, and repair physical damage. Men who can singlehandedly cause a fighter to win.)

1. Angelo Dundee
2. Ray Arcel
3. Whitey Bimstein
4. Gil Clancy
5. George Gainford
6. Chickie Ferrara
7. Charlie Goldman
8. Eddie Futch
9. Freddy Brown
10. Teddy Bentham-Jimmy August

CORNERMEN BRAVER THAN THEIR FIGHTERS

(These are the tough men who work corners and persistently send their fighters out for bigger and better beatings.)

1. Irving Ungerman (George Chuvalo)
2. Al Braverman (Chuck Wepner)
3. Cus D'Amato (Floyd Patterson)
4. Lou Gross (Al Jones)
5. Jack Quarry (Jerry Quarry)
6. Bruce Trampler (King of the four-rounders)
7. Paddy Flood (Bobby Cassidy)
8. Dick Sadler (George Foreman, Leon Spinks)
9. Ray Arcel (Hundreds of fighters)
10. Harry Kabakoff (King of the South-of-the-Border boxers)

Jim Pepe's Top 10 and Second 10 Fighters To Watch in the '80s

At 16, Jim Pepe has been avidly following boxing for four years. His dad, a sportswriter for the New York *Daily News,* frequently consults him when he needs boxing information.

THE TOP 10
(Listed in order of preference)

1. Tony Ayala, Jr., San Antonio, Tex., Junior middleweight—Only 17, already destroying tough veterans in the pros. At 14, nearly knocked out ex-WBA welterweight king Pepino Cuevas while sparring. A shoo-in to win a world title providing he calms down outside the ring. Nicknamed "Torito" or "Baby Bull," he stands only 5-7, yet has devastating power and excellent defensive skills. His amateur record was 140 wins, eight losses. After only six pro fights he was already ranked No. 23 in the world.
2. Johnny Bumphus, Nashville, Tenn., welterweight—As dazzling a fighter as you'll ever see, this lightning quick southpaw with good power to match, can also fight righthanded, switching sides with incredible ease. As an amateur, his weight fluctuated between 125 and 139 pounds, but he filled out to the 147-pound welterweight limit after only four pro fights. No. 1 U.S. amateur at 139 pounds, Johnny won a gold medal at the 1980 Olympic Trials and is a National AAU titleholder. A bright future is in store for this young man who recently turned pro under Top Rank, Inc.
3. Jackie Beard, Jackson, Tenn., bantamweight—Should Jackie ever decide to turn pro (something he has put off time and time again), it would probably be a smooth road to the title despite his lack of a knockout punch. Beard's defensive mastery and overall ability would more than make up for that one, albeit big, disadvantage. Beard was a 1980 U.S. Olympic Trials gold medal winner, holds three National AAU titles and was a gold medalist in the 1979 Pan American Games.
4. James Shuler, Philadelphia, middleweight—This no-nonsense young fighter out of Joe Frazier's gym has already established himself in the pros, scoring a couple of impressive early round stoppages. He has great concentration in the ring, no phony showboating, just business. Ranked No. 1 at 156 pounds before turning pro and a 1979 World Cup gold medalist, Shuler needs more activity against tougher opposition to sharpen his skills and then search for that title shot in two or three years.
5. Bernard Taylor, Charlotte, N.C., lightweight—Another

1980 Olympic Trials gold medalist, the multitalented Taylor, who holds an amateur victory over Johnny Bumphus in the 1977 Golden Gloves Tournament of Champions, recently turned pro under Top Rank. In his pro victories, his lack of punching power has hindered him somewhat, more so than Beard as an amateur, yet he still has the class, determination, and skill (plus a fine left jab) beyond his years which should eventually carry him to a championship. Bernard took a silver medal in the 1975 Pan American Games and a gold in the 1979 World Cup at Madison Square Garden.

6. Richard Sandoval, Pomona, Calif., bantamweight—This quick, clever boxer fought at 108 and 112 pounds as an amateur, but should fill out to the bantamweight limit of 118. Ranked No. 1 at 112 pounds before joining the punch-for-pay ranks, Rich won a gold medal at the 1979 World Cup and at the National AAU's, where he decisioned talented Jerome Coffee in the final. Sandoval's older brother, Alberto, was a world rated (No. 8) bantamweight before fading after earning a title shot. Rich should bring that championship home within a few years.
7. Mitchell Green, Jamaica, N.Y., heavyweight—Mitch, a tall and very quick fighter for a heavyweight, has already earned a few fine victories in the pro ranks, standing up to tough opposition very early in his career. A three-time New York Golden Gloves champion, including a one-round demolition of tough Guy Casale in 1977, Mitch was ranked third before turning pro. This bright, young prospect has a promising career ahead of him. Mitchell Green will win the world heavyweight championship within five years, and you can mark those words.
8. Tony Tucker, Grand Rapids, Mich., heavyweight—With every champion (Green) there is a No. 1 challenger, and this is the one. Instead of Dempsey-Tunney, or Ali-Frazier, it will be Green-Tucker in the 80s. Tony is a highly talented, long-armed, furious banger who took a gold at the 1979 World Cup and was ranked No. 1 prior to turning professional. Very strong

and determined, but Green barely edges him out on quickness.

9. Alex Ramos, Bronx, N.Y., middleweight—Tough, bull-like, muscular, and determined, Ramos is another multi-titled New York Golden Glover who had a style not well-suited for the amateur ranks. He is a strong infighter and will be able to use his head and shoulders in the pros, something frowned upon in the amateurs. Because of this, he lost many aggravating decisions in his latter amateur days, so he decided to turn pro, a smart decision. Ranked No. 6 at 156 pounds before turning pro, Alex will now be able to utilize his skills and prove his worth.
10. James Green, Irvington, N.J., middleweight—Unranked by most amateur rating bodies, this hard-hitting whirlwind burst into the limelight by stopping Alex Ramos in the New Yorker's last amateur fight. A National AAU runner-up ranked No. 3 before turning pro, James has accomplished something others only dream about—rave reviews from boxing's premier underground expert, "Flash" Gordon, who, after watching James's pro debut, proclaimed: "Watch this guy." Take heed to those words.

THE SECOND 10
(Listed alphabetically)

1. Jerome Coffee, Jackson, Tenn., flyweight—Ranked No. 2 before turning pro; very quick.
2. Donald Curry, Fort Worth, Tex., middleweight—Brother of contender Bruce Curry, '80 Olympic Trials winner, ranked No. 1 at 147 pounds.
3. Bobby Czyz, Wanaque, N.J., middleweight—24-2 as amateur, good stamina and a ferocious body puncher, now a pro under Lou Duva.
4. Marvis Frazier, Philadelphia, heavyweight—An extremely talented fighter aside from a glass jaw due to a recurring pinched nerve in the neck. Future very shaded following 23-second KO by slow James Broad in amateurs, being rocked several times in first few pro fights and getting knocked senseless in sparring session.

5. Ed Green, Ft. Bragg, N.C., welterweight—World Cup gold medalist, ranked No. 2 behind Curry, excellent footwork.
6. Milton McCrory, Detroit, welterweight—Trained by Emanuel Steward (Hearns, Kenty), tall, good power. Need I say more?
7. Patrizio Oliva, Italy, Junior middleweight—Olympic gold medalist (147 pounds), should win a title in this talent-poor weight class providing Tony Ayala moves up to middleweight.
8. Mike Sacchetti, Cleveland, middleweight—Unknown, unranked until beating pro-debuting Jeff Stoudemire, one of the nation's most highly regarded amateurs; a non-stop banger.
9. Jeff Stoudemire, Cleveland, middleweight—All-everything as an amateur, dropped pro debut but has seemingly bounced back well. Billed as "The Next Middleweight Champ."
10. Tony Tubbs, Santa Monica, Calif., heavyweight—Not much power, yet very quick and capable. World Cup gold medalist, No. 1 prior to turning pro.

Note: All pro rankings from *The Ring*'s International ratings. All amateur rankings from *The Amateur Boxer*.

Rusty Kanokogi's Top 10 All-Time U.S. Women Judo Competitors

Rusty Kanokogi is former coach of the United States women's judo team and was president of the organizing committee for the First Women's World Judo Championships in New York's Felt Forum in 1980.

1. Margaret Castro, New York
2. Maureen Braziel, New York
3. Delores Brodie, California
4. Lynne Lewis, Massachusetts
5. Amy Kublin, Massachusetts
6. Diane Pierce, Minnesota
7. Linda Richardson, Wisconsin

Coach Rusty Kanokogi demonstrates her judo techniques.

Sports Photo Source

8. Christine Penick, California
9. Mary Lewis, New York
10. Barbara Fest, Massachusetts

Pete Enich's 10 Best Collegiate Fight Songs

1. "The Victors" (Michigan)—Even Woody Hayes loves this song. It is a standard by which all pep songs should be measured.
2. "I'm A Jayhawk" (Kansas)—Gale Sayers, John Hadl, John Zook. The most beautiful campus in America. Memorial Stadium and the Jayhawk band.
3. "Minnesota Rouser" (Minnesota)—At one time the theme song for NCAA football telecasts.
4. "Mr. Touchdown U.S.A." (no school)—A tribute to all football heroes from eight to 80.
5. "On Mizzou" (Missouri)—The campus of beautiful women. Don Faurot, Paul Christman, Dan Devine, and the annual battle with Kansas.
6. "On Wisconsin" (Wisconsin)—The first "million seller" among fight songs. A solid favorite from coast to coast.
7. "Fight On" (Southern Cal)—Mike Garrett, O. J. Simpson, Ricky Bell, John Wayne. Football talent galore. A Trojan Warrior on a white horse.
8. "There Is No Place Like Nebraska" (Nebraska)—Midwest football at its very best. One of the snappiest tunes in the top 10.
9. "Across the Field" (Ohio State)—Bo Schembechler is not too fond of this tune. Shades of Hopalong Cassady, Rex Kern, Archie Griffin, and Ron Potamkin.
10. "Washington & Lee Swing" (Washington & Lee)—Aristocratic. Only Atlantic seaboard institution with a good fight song.

SOURCE: Kansas City *Kansan*.

Pete Enich's 10 Worst Collegiate Fight Songs

1. "Yea, Alabama" (Alabama)—Typically southern in style, which, translated, means blasé.
2. "The Eyes of Texas" (Texas)—Deliberate and dull, much like Darrell Royal's football teams. Bevo, the slow-moving longhorn.
3. "Iowa Corn Song" (Iowa)—The Hawkeyes have had no winners on the field or in the pep band since Alex Karras left.
4. "I've Been Working on the Railroad" (Colorado)—Finishes above the Kansas State song only because Buffalo officials had to plagiarize from an American heritage song to make this one bad.
5. "Wildcat Fight Song" (Kansas State)—A lullaby. Inspired Doug Weaver to an 8-60-1 football record in the '60s and drove Tex Winter to Northwestern.
6. "Boola-Boola" (Yale)—Quite overrated. No continuity, just like Eli football squads.
7. "The Sturdy Golden Bear" (California)—While this university has been on probation many times, the song hasn't. Perhaps NCAA officials should reconsider.
8. "The Cardinal Is Waving" (Stanford)—The mere title of this rhapsody should explain its inspirational qualities.
9. "She'll Be Comin' 'Round the Mountain" (SMU)—Guilty of the same transgression as Colorado, no originality. Graduate Lamar Hunt should commission a new songwriting team to hype up the Mustangs.
10. "The Olive and the Blue" (Tulane)—This fight song is atrocious. So were most of the teams fielded by Tulane in the last 30 years.

SOURCE: Kansas City *Kansan*.

Fascinating Nicknames of 77 American Colleges

1. Akron (Ohio) "Zips"

2. Alderson-Broaddus (W.Va.) "Battlers"
3. Amherst (Mass.) "Lord Jeffs"
4. Albany State (N.Y.) "Great Danes"
5. Arkansas-Monticello "Weevils"
6. Baltimore (Md.) "Super Bees"
7. Benthany (Kans.) "Terrible Swedes"
8. Bethel (Kans.) "Threshers"
9. Brandeis (Mass.) "Judges"
10. Cal-Irvine "Anteaters"
11. Colby (Me.) "White Mules"
12. Colorado Mines "Orediggers"
13. Cal. State-Sonoma "Cossacks"
14. Concordia (Minn.) "Cobblers"
15. Delaware "Blue Hens"
16. Dickinson State (N.D.) "Savages"
17. Emory & Henry (Va.) "Wasps"
18. Evansville (Ind.) "Purple Aces"
19. Furman (S.C.) "Paladins"
20. Glassboro State (N.J.) "Profs"
21. Hamline (Minn.) "Pipers"
22. Heidelberg (Ohio) "Student Princes"
23. Hofstra (N.Y.) "Flying Dutchmen"
24. Huron (S.D.) "Scalpers"
25. Idaho "Vandals"
26. John Carroll (Ohio) "Blue Streak"
27. Jersey City State (N.J.) "Gothics"
28. Kent State (Ohio) "Golden Flashes"
29. Kansas State-Pittsburg "Gorillas"
30. Lincoln Memorial (Tenn.) "Railsplitters"
31. Lemoyne-Owen (Tenn.) "Magicians"
32. Manhattan (N.Y.) "Jaspers"
33. Marshall (W.Va.) "Thundering Herd"
34. Marist (N.Y.) "Red Foxes"
35. Ohio Wesleyan "Battling Bishops"
36. Oberlin (Ohio) "Yeomen"
37. Oklahoma S&A "Drovers"
38. Oglethorpe (Ga.) "Stormy Petrels"
39. Pace (N.Y.) "Setters"
40. Presbyterian (S.C.) "Blue Hose"
41. Phillips (Okla.) "Haymakers"

42. Pomona-Pitzer (Calif.) "Sagehens"
43. Rollins (Fla.) "Tars"
44. Rhode Island College "Anchormen"
45. Roosevelt (Ill.) "Torchbearers"
46. St. Louis (Mo.) "Billikens"
47. South Dakota "Coyotes"
48. South Dakota State "Jackrabbits"
49. Southern Illinois-Carbondale "Salukis"
50. Stetson (Fla.) "Hatters"
51. Southwest Louisiana "Ragin' Cajuns"
52. Southwestern (Tenn.) "Lynx"
53. St. Joseph's (Me.) "Monks"
54. South Dakota Tech "Hardrockers"
55. Southern State (Ark.) "Muleriders"
56. San Diego (Calif.) "Toreros"
57. Tufts (Mass.) "Jumbos"
58. Trinity (Vt.) "Bantams"
59. Thiel (Pa.) "Tomcats"
60. Thomas Jefferson (Pa.) "Medics"
61. Virginia Tech "Gobblers"
62. Virginia Wesleyan "Blue Marlins"
63. Wake Forest (N.C.) "Demon Deacons"
64. Wichita State (Kans.) "Wheatshockers"
65. Wisconsin—Green Bay "Fighting Phoenix"
66. Williams (Mass.) "Ephmen"
67. Wayne State (Mich.) "Tartars"
68. Westminster (Utah) "Parsons"
69. Washburn (Kans.) "Ichabods"
70. Whittier (Calif.) "Poets"
71. Wabash (Ind.) "Little Giants"
72. Whitman (Wash.) "Missionaries"
73. Western Maryland "Green Terrors"
74. Wisconsin—Stevens Point "Pointers"
75. Washington (Mo.) "Shoremen"
76. Western Illinois "Leathernecks"
77. Xavier (Ohio) "Musketeers"

Submitted by Dan Maschino, Dayton, Ohio.

This was at Forest Hills, New York, in 1956 when Ken Rosewall won the U.S. Nationals.

UPI

Lobs and Links

Lance Tingay's 10 Greatest Tennis Upsets

Lance Tingay has been covering tennis for the London *Daily Telegraph* for almost half a century.

1. Ken Rosewall defeated Lew Hoad, 4-6, 6-2, 6-3, 6-3, in the finals of the 1956 U.S. National men's singles championship, Forest Hills. (Hoad was lined up for the Grand Slam, having won the Australian title by beating Rosewall in the final; the French, beating Sven Davidson, and Wimbledon, beating Rosewall. It was Rosewall, Hoad's doubles partner, who ruined the chance for the Slam.)
2. Charles Pasarell beat Manuel Santana, 10-8, 6-3, 2-6, 8-6, in the first round of the Wimbledon championships, 1967. (It marked the only time the defending champion and top seed was beaten in the opening round at Wimbledon.)
3. Mark Cox beat Pancho Gonzales, 0-6, 6-2, 4-6, 6-3, 6-3, British Hard Court Championships, Bournemouth, men's singles, second round, 1968. (At the world's first open championship, the amateur Cox humbled the mighty Gonzales, reckoned as one of the greatest of all time and the most heavyweight of all the professionals.)
4. Kay Stammers beat Helen Wills Moody, 6-0, 6-4, at Beckenham, Kent Championships, semifinals, women's singles, 1935. (The first defeat suffered by the invincible Mrs. Moody since 1927.)

5. Nigel Sharpe beat Henri Cochet, 6-1, 6-3, 6-2, at Wimbledon, first round, men's singles, 1931. (Probably the most abysmal of Cochet's defeats. The French genius had been Wimbledon champion in 1927 and 1929 and was seeded number two. Sharpe had the greatest win of his career, by far.)
6. Jennifer Middleton and Doreen Spiers beat top seeds Doris Hart and Barbara Davidson, 6-4, 1-6, 6-2, Wimbledon, women's doubles, second round, 1956. (Probably the most inexplicable outcome in the history of women's doubles.)
7. Christine Truman beat Althea Gibson, 2-6, 6-3, 6-4, Wightman Cup, Wimbledon, 1958. (The vital rubber by which Great Britain beat the United States for the first time since 1930. The 17-year-old Christine Truman brought down the unquestioned number one woman in the world.)
8. Billie Jean Moffit beat Margaret Smith, 1-6, 6-3, 7-5, Wimbledon, women's singles, second round, 1962. (Margaret Smith was the top seed and was beaten in her opening match by the 18-year-old California novice.)
9. Ismail El Shafei beat Bjorn Borg, 6-2, 6-3, 6-1, Wimbledon, men's singles, third round, 1974. (Borg could not get off the Centre Court fast enough.)
10. Jan Kodes beat John Newcombe, 2-6, 7-6, 7-6, 6-3, U.S. Open Championships, men's singles, first round, Forest Hills, 1971. (This was on grass and Kodes had just said it was fit only for cows. Newcombe was the number one seed.)

Edwin Pope's 10 Greatest Golfers

1. Jack Nicklaus
2. Ben Hogan
3. Sam Snead
4. Gary Player
5. Arnold Palmer
6. Byron Nelson
7. Bobby Jones
8. Walter Hagen
9. Gene Sarazen
10. Lee Trevino

Jack Nicklaus blasts his way to the 1980 PGA championship in Rochester.
Wide World

Danny Lawler's 6 Best Golfing Baseball Players in Each Facet of the Game

The "golf pro of the major leaguers," Danny Lawler was golf pro at Rock Ridge Country Club in Newtown, Conn. Currently, he does public relations for Izod sportswear.

1. Driver—Jim Rice
2. Long Irons—Tommy John
3. Middle Irons—Don Zimmer
4. Short Irons—Dick Howser
5. Sand Trap— Rick Cerone
6. Putter—Jim Palmer

Jim Palmer doesn't throw curves when he's putting.
American Airlines/Sports Photo Source

The 25 Best Golf Courses Outside the United States

Says Peter Dobereiner, who compiled this list for *Golf Digest:* "Anyone who sets out to compile merit lists, be they of the world's 10 most beautiful women, the seven deadliest sins, the 20 finest works of art, or the best golf courses outside the United States, lays himself open to charges of prejudice, ignorance, folly and corruption. So be it. Let the accusations fly. The defendant pleads guilty on all counts except that of bribery, all opportunities for which were sadly absent from the exercise.

"If personal preferences mean prejudice, then the list is prejudiced. If something less than an intimate knowledge of every golf course in the world means ignorance, then the list is ignorant. And if undue emphasis on an especially delightful feature of an otherwise ordinary course means folly, then the rankings in some places are foolish."

The courses, in order of preference:

1. Royal County Down, Newcastle, Northern Ireland—Magnificent links on Dundrum Bay with the Mountains of Mourne sweeping down to the sea, formed in 1899. Architect: Tom Morris.
2. Royal Melbourne, Australia—All the natural forces of weather, topography, vegetation, and subsoil combine to make the Melbourne sand belt perfect golfing country and Royal Melbourne is the best of an outstanding bunch. Smoothest greens anywhere. Architect: Alistair Mackenzie.
3. Durban Country Club, Natal, South Africa—Rolling sand hills, lush tropical vegetation, cooling sea breezes, and an exceptional layout that has stood the test of time since 1920. Architect: Laurie Walters.
4. Cajuiles, La Romana, Dominican Republic—One of the few masterpieces of modern golf. Architect: Pete Dye.
5. El Saler, Valencia, Spain—Seaside golf at its best, combined with a very special Spanish flavor. Architect: Javier Arana.
6. Muirfield, East Lothian, Scotland—Possibly the oldest club in the world, a traditional links and the fairest of

them all, with hazards clearly visible and splendid views across the Firth of Forth. Architect: unknown.

7. Hirono, Kobe, Japan—Predates the great Japanese golfing explosion, having been built in 1932, and it therefore served as a model and an inspiration for those that followed. Architect: C.H. Alison.
8. Lagunita, Caracas, Venezuela—Another park course, relatively short by championship standards at less than 7,000 yards, but its superb design makes it a tough proposition for the best. Architect: Dick Wilson.
9. Royal Birkdale, Southport, England—Nature is the true architect of Birkdale, with huge sand hills dictating the character of the holes. A tenacious variety of willow scrub makes a unique rough which can break your heart if not your club. Architect: Fred Hawtree.
10. Dorado Beach, Puerto Rico—If the developer has enough cash and the architect has enough imagination, anything is possible, as Dorado Beach proves. Once a mosquito-infested swamp, it is now a millionaire-infested golfing playground. Architect: Robert Trent Jones.
11. Royal Montreal, Canada—Another uncompromising site transformed into a glorious course on which the designer unashamedly invites the golfer to pause and admire the views during his progress along the fairways. Architect: Dick Wilson.
12. Kasumigaseki, Tokyo, Japan—With not a blade of grass out of place, it seems almost profane to play golf on such lovingly and lavishly manicured terrain. But well worth it, for this is Japanese golf at its very best. Architects: Kinja Fujita and C. H. Alison.
13. Ballybunion, County Kerry, Ireland—You cannot get farther away from it all than this wild and glorious stretch of Atlantic duneland, nearly always to be played in a spanking wind with the tang of peat smoke in your nostrils and always in gratitude at being alive. Architect: unknown.
14. Nchanga, Chingola, Zambia—You have never heard of it? Sadly, few can ever see it, but this jungle course built by copper miners is rated by Bobby Locke as the finest

course south of the equator. Great golf, plus botanical garden, plus safari park. Architect: unknown.

15. Walton Heath, Surrey, England—Although the majestic design has been slightly modified by tampering committees and intrusive roadbuilding, Walton Heath remains one of Britain's glories of inland golf. Architect: Herbert Fowler.
16. Club zur Vahr, Bremen, Germany—Carved through a forest of massive conifers, Vahr combines a superb strategic layout, demanding the widest variety of shots. Architect: Bernard von Limburger.
17. New South Wales, G.C., Matraville, Australia—Very tough, very attractive and mostly very windy. The golf here is enhanced by the bonus of sea views over the Pacific and Botany Bay. Architect: Alistair Mackenzie.
18. Penina, Algarve, Portugal—A monster off the back tees, but swallow your pride and move forward and the course becomes a delight. Architect: Henry Cotton.
19. Club de Golf Mexico, Mexico City—Definitely one for tree lovers, it cuts its way through groves of cypresses, eucalyptus, pine and cedar. Architects: Percy J. Clifford and Laurence Hughes.
20. Den Haag, Netherlands—Justly proud of its reputation as the best links course in continental Europe, The Hague has switchback fairways and some of the most undulating greens to be found anywhere, making golf a sometimes frustrating, but always rewarding experience. Architect: Sir Guy Campbell.
21. Great Harbour Cay, Bahamas—Unashamedly a resort course, it is an outstanding example of the genre in the idyllic surroundings of a tiny Caribbean island with golf muted to a holiday mood. Architect: Joe Lee.
22. Pevero, Sardinia, Italy—A resort for wealthy holiday makers, but what a tiger of a course for a poor, tired businessman. Blasted out of the boulders and scrub of the macchia country, where brigands once hid from the law. A stray shot spells a lost ball. Magnificent golf. Architect: Robert Trent Jones.
23. Wack Wack, Manila, Philippines—A decent, honest course with a well-deserved international reputation,

Wack Wack was named after the cry of the crows which formerly nested there and not, as many assume, from a caddie's description of his master's efforts. Architect: Jim Black.

24. Banff Springs, Alberta, Canada—Surely the most spectacular course in the world, set among the Rockies and positively defying the golfer to keep his eye on the ball. The scenery often obscures the fact that the course is superb in its own right. Architect: Stanley Thompson.
25. Royal Johannesburg, South Africa—This is flattering golf for the ball flies great distances in the rarefied atmosphere of the high Rand, but it is also humiliating golf, save for the trusty few, because the notorious nap makes putts break uphill. Architect: R. G. Grimsdell.

XI

Hoofbeats

Arlene Francis' 10 Most Beautiful Horses

An original panelist on "What's My Line," Arlene Francis was a regular on that long-running, eminently successful television show. Currently, she is the hostess of "The Arlene Francis Show" on WOR radio in New York. She and her husband, actor Martin Gabel, are owners of horses. "This is not a critical analysis, it's sentimental," says Arlene. "Beauty is in the eye of the beholder."

1. Secretariat
2. Man 'O War—"From his pictures; I'm too young."
3. Equipoise
4. Swaps
5. Affirmed
6. Alydar
7. Arlene Francis—"I'm a chauvinist."
8. Damascus—"Arlene Francis' brother."
9. Genuine Risk
10. Ruffian

Francis adds: "At least I didn't include 'my son' by Le Fabuleux, Fabulous Find, who won his maiden just like Arlene Francis."

Bill Christine's 10 Most-Memorable Walkovers in Thoroughbred Racing History

Bill Christine is assistant to the executive vice president of the Thoroughbred Racing Associations, a trade organization of 53 tracks in the United States and Canada, which is located in Lake Success, N.Y. Before joining the TRA, Christine worked as a newspaperman in East St. Louis, Ill., Baltimore, Louisville, Chicago, and Pittsburgh. He is the author of "Roberto!" a biography of the late Hall of Fame outfielder, Roberto Clemente.

Says Christine: "A walkover in horse racing is the equivalent of a forfeit. The opponents don't show up, either because of fear or good sense, and the remaining opponent is the winner, providing the horse still negotiates the course as scheduled. Officially, this is the way the Rules of Racing define a walkover: 'When two horses in entirely different interests do not run for a race . . . In a case of a walkover, one-half of the money offered to the winner is given.' Which is why Spectacular Bid, who won the 1980 Woodward Stakes at Belmont Park in the first walkover in flat racing in 31 years, earned only $73,300 in what was scheduled as a $200,000-added race.

"Eclipse, the great English racehorse and foundation sire of the 18th century, went undefeated in his 26-race career, and he so dominated the thoroughbreds of his time that eight of the victories were walkovers.

"On the flat and in jump races, there have been more than 30 walkovers in the United States in this century. The 10 most famous follow."

1. Spectacular Bid, Woodward Stakes, Belmont Park, 1980—The last race in the career of the great colt, who finished with 26 victories out of 30 starts and record lifetime earnings of $2,781,607.
2. Coaltown, Edward Burke Handicap, Havre de Grace, Maryland, 1949—Second to his stablemate, Citation, in the Kentucky Derby the year before, Coaltown was assigned 130 pounds for the Edward Burke, and no other owner thought that this was enough weight to stop him.
3. Citation, Pimlico Special, Pimlico Race Course, 1948—The Triple Crown champion won $10,000 for this walk-

Spectacular Bid, with Willie Shoemaker aboard, leaves the starting gate for his solo at Belmont Park in 1980.

Wide World

over, tying a record for this type of race which stood until Spectacular Bid in 1980. The Pimlico Special was an invitational, and none of the other 24 invitees accepted, in part because at the time there was no purse share allocated to runners-up.

4. Stymie, Saratoga Cup, Saratoga Race Course, 1946—George Cassidy, who has been a part of New York racing since 1929, has served as the official starter for nine walkovers in his career. "Stymie came out of the

gate and ran just a bit," Cassidy remembers. "Then he stuck his toes in the ground. Hirsch Jacobs (the owner and trainer of Stymie) was worried that the horse wouldn't make it around the course."

5. Whirlaway, Pimlico Special, Pimlico Race Course, 1942—Although Alsab, who was to win the 3-year old championship this year, had defeated the 4-year old Whirlaway, 1941 Triple Crown winner, by a nose in a match race six weeks before, Alsab skipped the Pimlico race in favor of the richer Westchester Handicap in New York. Whirlaway took the $10,000 purse, then a walkover record, as the other 18 invitees declined.
6. Exterminator, Saratoga Cup, Saratoga Race Course, 1921—Exterminator, who won 50 races in his lifetime, won 11 of 13 overall at distances of 1¾ miles and farther. "Old Bones," as he was called, had also won this race twice before the walkover. The second-place purse of $1,000, an estimable sum in these times, went begging.
7. Roamer, Autumn Stakes, Belmont Park, 1914—Roamer, who became the year's top 3-year old after Kentucky Derby winner Old Rosebud went lame, may be the only walkover victor who had to run the course twice. Through a starter's error, Roamer ran the wrong way the first time—15 years before Roy Riegels and 24 years before Corrigan.
8. Purchase, Jockey Club Stakes, Belmont Park, 1919—Named after the Westchester County (N.Y.) community where his owner, George Smith, lived, Purchase had previously beaten Sir Barton, first winner of the Triple Crown, by three lengths.
9. Questionnaire and Awake, Mount Kisco Stakes, Empire City, New York, 1930—This was a two-horse race, but still considered a walkover since both runners raced in the colors of James Butler.
10. Isolator and Fenelon, Saratoga Cup, Saratoga Race Course, 1940—Another two-horse walkover, with the Belair Stud's entry completing the course after Challedon, who would still be named Horse of the Year, came down with colic the night before the race.

10A. Secretariat, Belmont Stakes, Belmont Park, 1973—This wasn't really a walkover, of course, although photos of the finish made it appear to be. Secretariat defeated a four-horse field by a remarkable 31 lengths to complete his sweep of the Triple Crown.

Andy Furman's 15 Promotional Stunts for Monticello Raceway, One of Which Got Him Fired

1. Prison Night—I sent a letter to the wardens at area prisons in Naponach and Woodburne Correctional Institutions for a night at the races. Never came off. Did get a real nice reply from the warden at Woodburne asking for a donation. He said the State of New York wouldn't let "the boys" out for racing . . . or anything else, for that matter.
2. Funeral Directors Night—All area funeral directors were sent invitations to the race track and a "lucky" fan would receive a free casket and funeral should his lucky number be picked from the daily racing program. Directors came and we had a coffin, but we didn't raffle it off. The track president thought it too morbid. He was afraid after some heavy losses that night a fan might decide to use it on the spot.
3. Giant Night—The Football Giants were invited to the track. Beasley Reece, the "fastest strong safety in the NFL," raced 7-year-old pacer Super Kris. Reece won. Super Kris was 0-for-73 before that race. Oh, yes, all those seven feet or taller were admitted free.
4. Diamond Night—A $2,000, three-quarter carat stone was purchased and distributed along with 4,000 glass look-alikes to the first 4,000 women that entered the track. The real winner never came forth to let the track personnel know. Probably afraid of the IRS.
5. Black Cat Night—On Friday, June 13, the first 50 entrants were given a black cat. Forgot to mention to media that they were toy cats. Created many problems

with the SPCA and local and regional humane society people.

6. Elephantonian Day—Harness racing's answer to the Hambletonian. Two live elephants raced a quarter mile on the track. One problem. We advertised the fact that the elephants were pacers. We were shipped trotters. No betting on this event.
7. Phemonenal Peddle Pace—We had three harness drivers race on 10-speed bicycles for a quarter mile. Gary Messenger, one of the track's leading drivers, took a spill after his bike got a flat tire. No wagering.
8. Best Looking Day—The Playboy Club in McAfee, N.J., supplied the bunnies to choose the Monticello Raceway best-looking driver-trainer. Problem: People too busy judging the judges.
9. Guaranteed Win Night—Every Monday, all those who stayed after the last race and wanted to pick up the losing ticket stubs at the track were awarded free french fries at the Monticello (N.Y.) Burger King.
10. Ban Russian Horse Day—A letter was sent to the Russian premier, Brezhnev, informing him that Monticello Raceway would, in fact, support President Carter's Olympic boycott and ban all Russian horses from racing at Monticello Raceway.
11. George Burns Day—A letter was sent to George, along with some cigars, inviting him to sing the national anthem on Opening Day, May 1, 1980. He was too busy playing God.
12. Rosie Ruiz Day—A race named after the New Yorker who finished first among women in the 1980 Boston Marathon, but was later stripped of the title for allegedly having cut the course short. Our race would have no starting or finish line. This was canceled when her lawyer replied, informing us she would not be interested.
13. Polish Night—Mighty M had the world's largest kielbasa, and every fan got a piece upon entering the track. Polish Pace consisted of a backwards pace and loser paid off. Program was listed in reverse order.
14. Twin Night—All identical twins admitted free.

15. KKK Night—This is the one that did me in. A letter was sent to the local KKK chapter to invite them for a day at the track. Media picked it up and track officials panicked. Hence, I was asked to leave.

Eddie Arcaro's 5 Greatest Horses

1. Kelso
2. Citation—"Best three-year-old I ever rode."
3. Ribot—"The best foreign horse I ever saw."
4. Assault
5. Forego

SOURCE: *Inside Sports.*

Jim Bolus' Favorite Boo-Boo Racing Finishes

Jim Bolus of The Louisville *Times* and former publicity director at Churchill Downs, is the author of *Run for the Roses,* a history of the Kentucky Derby.

1. A Nightmare Finish—During the week of the 1957 Kentucky Derby, owner Ralph Lowe had a dream. He dreamed that his colt, Gallant Man, was charging down the stretch in the Derby, on his way to certain victory, when his rider misjudged the finish line and pulled up prematurely, costing his horse the race.

   Jockey Bill Shoemaker, informed of the dream, told Lowe not to worry about a thing. Then Shoemaker went out and stood up at the 16th pole and Gallant Man lost by a nose to Iron Liege.
2. Wake Up, Rip—The same Shoemaker, who would go on to become the winningest jockey of all, would have had another victory had he not relaxed on Swaps in the homestretch of the 1956 Californian Stakes. Swaps seemed to have the race won, but Porterhouse came with a rush to triumph by a head.

   Both *The Blood-Horse* and *The Thoroughbred Record* accused Shoemaker of going to sleep aboard Swaps. The

Record's Leon Rasmussen observed: "Shoemaker, actually, was merely napping. But since a nap has been described as 'brief period of sleep,' the jockey Rip Van Winkled Swaps and himself out of a $63,700 pot."

3. First Goof—For a man who led American jockeys in total victories in 1945 and reportedly had NEVER made a mistake in a race, Job Jessop was guilty of one in the 1946 Kentucky Derby. He misjudged the finish line aboard third-place finisher Hampden, who wasn't going to get close to Assault, an eight-length victor. But if it hadn't been for Jessop's boo-boo, Hampden stood a good chance of finishing second ahead of Spy Song.
4. Let's See . . . One, Two, Three—Eddie Arcaro was known as "Heady Eddie" and "The Master." But he had trouble with his arithmetic in the 1949 Pimlico Cup. He had the mount on Blue Hills. The race was two miles and a half. With Blue Hills leading after the first mile and a half, Arcaro eased up on his mount. After realizing his mistake, Arcaro went back to riding, but the best Blue Hills could do was finish second, beaten eight lengths by Pilaster.

   "I didn't know that it wasn't the finish until I started to pull up and the other horses went by me," said Arcaro. "Then Jimmy Lynch, who rode Bayeux, hollered, 'We have to go around again, buddy.' I guess I'll have to go back to school and learn to count."
5. No No, Sweet William—Bill Hartack misjudged the Churchill Downs finish line in 1974. Yes, the same Hartack who won the 1957 Derby with Iron Liege after Shoemaker misjudged the finish line aboard Gallant Man. It happened in the National Turf Writers Association Purse and, interestingly, there was a clear message for Hartack in this race—if he had only paid attention to the winner's name.

   Hartack, it seems, stood up just inside the 16th pole aboard Fun Co K., who was leading. The horse who was running second at that point proceeded to pass Fun Co K. and win the race by a head. All Hartack had to do was look back just before the 16th pole and ask that horse his name. It was No No Billy.

6. So Who's Perfect?—Riding Nodouble in the 1968 Preakness, William McKeever stood up in the irons for at least one stride at the 16th pole. McKeever claimed that Nodouble "was trying to throw a shoe. He hobbled and I started to pull him up."

   The stewards, however, didn't see it that way and, after studying the patrol films, they fined McKeever $100 for misjudging the finish line on Nodouble, who was moved up from fourth to third on a disqualification.

   McKeever subsequently explained. "Well, how should I know where the finish line is? I've never rid here before."
7. Did He or Didn't He?—Colin, who finished his career with an unbeaten record, won the 1908 Belmont Stakes by a head over Fair Play. The chart of the race stated that Joe Notter, who rode Colin, misjudged the finish line. The jockey denied it. One account noted that the horse was having tendon trouble and had attempted to ease himself. "Colin misjudged that finish," Notter was quoted as saying. "I didn't."
8. For Cripes Sake—The Churchill Downs stretch played tricks on jockey J. Rosello in 1965. He stood up near the 16th pole and finished second aboard Sir Bop in a mistake that might or might not have cost him the victory. As Bob Hurley of the *Daily Racing Form* put it, "Any jockey with a first name like Rosello's should be entitled to one mistake."

   His first name? Jesus.
9. Two Blind Mice—It happened in an 1899 race at New York's Morris Park. The 1 ¾-mile event brought together a small field of three. "It was to have been run over the Withers course," reported *The New York Times*, "and when the first quarter had been run, Slack on Julius Caesar, who was in front, sent his mount off the Withers course and showed the way up the course that led over the hill. Wilson, on the favorite Maid of Harlem, knew the course he was to ride, and went on over the Withers, but Odom, on Spurs, followed Julius Caesar blindly until he had traveled a quarter of a mile on the wrong course, and then realizing that a mistake

had been made, he went back and took his mount over the proper course. Spurs got second money . . . but Julius Caesar ran on over the hill course and was not given third money."

The stewards fined Slack and Odom $100 each and the trainers of the two horses $50 each for failure to instruct the jockeys which course to take.

Edwin Pope's 10 Greatest Jockeys

1. Eddie Arcaro
2. Willie Shoemaker
3. Bill Hartack
4. Angel Cordero
5. Ted Atkinson
6. Walter Blum
7. Bob Ussery
8. Johnny Longden
9. Jorge Velasquez
10. Howard Grant

11 Athletes Who Have Owned Harness Horses

1. Charlie Keller
2. Ingemar Johansson
3. Whitey Ford
4. Mickey Mantle
5. Wilt Chamberlain
6. Dan Issel
7. Giles Villemure
8. John Ferguson
9. Bobby Hull
10. Arnold Palmer
11. Lew Worsham

Submitted by Mark A. Williams from information obtained from *Hoofbeats Magazine*.

Patrick M. Premo's 10 Greatest American Quarterhorses and 10 Greatest American Appaloosas of All Time

A horse racing buff since he was 15, Patrick M. Premo is professor of accounting at St. Bonaventure University and a CPA who developed a strategy horse racing game called "They're Off," which features over 200 all-time great thoroughbreds, harness horses, and quarterhorses. He has written for such magazines as *The Speedhorse, The Appaloosa*

Eddie Arcaro won the Kentucky Derby five times.

Charlie Williams

Racing Record, All-Star Replay, Table Top Sports, and *All-Sports Digest*. His lists are chronological, by year foaled.

QUARTERHORSES

1. Shu Fly*, 1937
2. Miss Princess*/Woven Web**, 1943
3. Maddon's Bright Eyes*, 1946
4. Go Man Go, 1953
5. Jet Deck, 1960
6. Easy Jet, 1967
7. Easy Date*, 1972
8. Tiny's Gay, 1972
9. Dash For Cash, 1973
10. Moon Lark, 1976

APPALOOSAS

1. Apache King S., 1959
2. Ledge Deck, 1966
3. Miss Go Go Kid*, 1966
4. My Host Bright*, 1966
5. E2's Absarokee Maid*, 1967
6. Star Diver, 1968
7. Apache Double, 1969
8. Time Flies, 1971
9. We Go Easy*, 1973
10. The Hooper Honker, 1975

Official quarterhorse records were not kept until the early 1940s; official racing Appaloosa records were not kept until the early 1960s.

* Designates filly/mare.

** Woven Web was actually a thoroughbred who was known on the quarter tracks as Miss Princess.

XII

The Great and the Powerful

David A. (Sonny) Werblin's 12 Greatest Sports Promoters of All Time

As the "creator" of the Joe Namath legend, which put the American Football League on the map, Sonny Werblin knows a good promoter when he sees one. Werblin is currently President and Chief Executive Officer of Madison Square Garden Corporation.

1. Doc Kearns, boxing
2. Bill Veeck, baseball
3. Tex Rickard, Madison Square Garden
4. Abe Saperstein, Harlem Globetrotters
5. Muhammad Ali/Howard Cosell, a partnership
6. Eddie Gottlieb, founder, National Basketball Association
7. Paul Bear Bryant, college football
8. George Halas, co-founder, National Football League
9. Mike Jacobs, boxing

Bill Veeck, right, plays the fife in a Spirit of '76 bicentennial ceremony in Chicago.
UPI

10. Lamar Hunt, tennis
11. Ned Irish, basketball
12. Leo Seltzer, roller derby

Pat Harmon's 25 Greatest Sports Achievements in Cincinnati History

"Can any other city the size of Cincinnati match a list like this?" asks Pat Harmon, sports editor of the Cincinnati *Post*.

1. Reds beat Phillies in three, Yankees in four, to become the only baseball team to sweep both the playoffs and World Series, 1976.
2. Johnny Vander Meer's two successive no-hitters, 1938.
3. Wishing Ring wins at Latonia and pays $1,885.50, still a world record for a $2 mutuel ticket on a single horse, 1912.
4. University of Cincinnati wins two consecutive NCAA basketball tournaments, 1961-62.
5. Pete Rose gets 3,000 hits, wins three batting titles, has a record 44-game hitting streak, in 16 years with the Reds, 1963-78.
6. DeHart Hubbard wins the long jump; first black athlete to win an Olympic gold medal, 1924.
7. Tony Trabert wins Wimbledon, U.S. and French singles, 1955.
8. Four world professional boxing champions. They are, with years they won titles: Freddie Miller, featherweight, 1934; Ezzard Charles, heavyweight, 1949; Bud Smith, lightweight, 1955; Aaron Pryor, junior welterweight, 1980.
9. Darrell Pace wins two world championships, six nationals and one Olympic in archery, 1973-80.
10. Jockey Steve Cauthen (from nearby Kentucky) wins the Triple Crown on Affirmed, 1978.
11. Xavier wins the National Invitation Tournament, upsetting Dayton, the No. 1 seed, Bradley, No. 2, and St. Bonaventure, No. 3, 1953.
12. Reds win the World Series and every Red says it was on the level, 1919 (year of the Black Sox scandal).
13. Reds have three straight MVPs—Ernie Lombardi, 1938; Bucky Walters, 1939; Frank McCormick, 1940.
14. Nancy Vonderheide wins the women's world archery title, 1961.

One of Johnny Vander Meer's two consecutive no-hitters for Cincinnati occurred in the first night game in New York City history—at Brooklyn's Ebbets Field in 1938.

UPI

15. Henry Holtgrewe wins world weight-lifting title, 1904.
16. Walter Laufer outswims Johnny Weissmuller, 1926.
17. Johnny Fischer wins the National Amateur Golf tournament, 1936.
18. Oscar Robertson sets Madison Square Garden scoring record, 1958.
19. Clang beats Myrtlewood in match race, sets world record for six furlongs, at Coney Island Race Track,

As a collegian, Cincinnati's Oscar Robertson drew capacity crowds, as he did here against NYU at Madison Square Garden in 1958. A season earlier, as a sophomore, Oscar scored 56 points against Seton Hall for a Garden record.

UPI

now River Downs, 1935.

20. Cincinnati Central Y wins national YMCA basketball tournament four times in six years, 1923-28.
21. Reds beat Boston Red Sox in seven-game World Series, called by many "the greatest Series ever played," 1975.
22. Indianapolis suspends the 500-mile Memorial Day race and Cincinnati takes the date with the top drivers competing. Louis Chevrolet beats out Barney Oldfield, Ira Vail, Gaston Chevrolet, Tommy Milton, Ralph DePalma. Attendance, 60,000, Cincinnati's all-time sports crowd, 1917.
23. Wintergreen, bred and raced by Rome Respess at his Woodlawn horse farm in northern Cincinnati, wins the Kentucky Derby, 1912.
24. Reds draw 2,629,708, better than five times the population of the city, 1976.
25. Paul Brown's Bengals win a division of the NFL in only the third year of the franchise, a record for an expansion team, 1970.

Mary Flannery's 11 Most Influential Women on New York's Sports Scene

Mary Flannery is a sportswriter for the New York *Daily News.*

1. Pat Kennedy—She and her husband started a girls' basketball summer camp under her name in 1966. Now it's a cross-country network. With the Kennedy-Levy sports promotion firm, she handles the Wade Trophy and the Manufacturers Hanover Christmas Classic at Madison Square Garden.
2. Billie Jean King—The original fighter, she hasn't unlaced her gloves yet.
3. Lucille Kyvallos—When women's basketball was on the ground level, she was there at Queens College. After 12 years, she resigned as coach, a casualty of low pay and the exhaustive struggle.
4. Nancy Lieberman—Next to Bill Walton, basketball's best known redhead. She was the No. 1 pick overall in the 1980 Women's Basketball League draft. The three-

Billie Jean King gets ready to settle a score with Bobby Riggs in their "Battle of the Sexes." Billie Jean dispatched Riggs and won $100,000.

ABC/Sports Photo Source

time Kodak All-America signed a three-year, $50,000 per contract with the Dallas Diamonds.

5. Edy McGoldrick—Vice president of Capital Sports, Inc., a promotional marketing corporation. She parlayed her savvy from her years as a department store buyer and her tennis connections from Wightman Cup days. One of her projects is to convince the Women's Tennis Association to hold its own U.S. Open.
6. Ellie Riger—The first woman to produce a live college football game, Colorado State-Wyoming. Since then, she has produced 40 for ABC-TV, a score of "Wide World of Sports" shows and two prime-time specials.

7. Sue Sedlacek—The most successful female horse trainer in New York. In 1980, she had 241 starters and 106 finished in the money, with purses totaling $528,232.
8. Kathrine Switzer—Special promotions manager for Avon Products, she helped convince international track and field bodies to include a women's marathon in the Olympics.
9. Margaret Wigiser—Supervisor of the girls' branch of New York City's Public Schools Athletic League with 15,000 girls competing in 10 varsity sports at 100 high schools. "Nancy Lieberman was one of ours," she proudly points out.
10. Sister Febronia, C.S.J.—President of the Girls' Catholic High School Athletic Association for the diocese of Brooklyn.
11. Jane Morris—Sister Febronia's counterpart for the New York archdiocese.

The 25 Greatest Athletes of All Time

Selected in a poll of the nation's top sportswriters and broadcasters conducted by the Miller Brewing Company.

ATHLETE	SPORT	POINTS
1. Babe Ruth	Baseball	111
2. Muhammad Ali	Boxing	106
3. Jim Brown	Football	92
4. Jack Nicklaus	Golf	91
5. Jim Thorpe	Football, track and field	88
6. Joe DiMaggio	Baseball	86
7. (tie) Arnold Palmer	Golf	81
O.J. Simpson	Football	81
9. (tie) Wilt Chamberlain	Basketball	79
Mark Spitz	Swimming	79
11. (tie) Jesse Owens	Track & Field	76

Lacrosse was another sport of Jim Brown's at Syracuse.
Syracuse/Sports Photo Source

Jim Thorpe as a New York Giant in 1917.
UPI

	Joe Louis	Boxing	76
13.	(tie) Ty Cobb	Baseball	75
	Bill Russell	Basketball	75
15.	Henry Aaron	Baseball	74
16.	(tie) Willie Mays	Baseball	63
	Babe Didrickson Zaharias	Golf	63
18.	Ted Williams	Baseball	62
19.	Red Grange	Football	58
20.	Pelé	Soccer	57
21.	Billie Jean King	Tennis	56
22.	Gordie Howe	Hockey	49

Jack Dempsey cut quite a figure in 1917—
two years before he knocked out Jess
Willard to win the heavyweight title.
Sports Photo Source

23. (tie) A.J. Foyt	Auto racing	47
Johnny Unitas	Football	47
25. Bjorn Borg	Tennis	44

Elliott Denman's 10 Greatest New Jersey Athletes

Elliott Denman is a sportswriter for the Asbury Park (N.J.) *Press.*

1. Milton Campbell
2. Jersey Joe Walcott
3. Renaldo (Skeets) Nehemiah
4. Paul Robeson
5. Al Blozis
6. John Borican
7. Dick Button
8. Horace Ashenfelter
9. Don (Tarzan) Bragg
10. Willie Wilson

Joe Lapchick's Greatest Athletes of All Time in 8 Sports

Joe Lapchick, the legendary basketball coach for the New York Knicks and St. John's University, jotted these names down on the program of a sports dinner just before his death in 1970 for Bill Gallo, sports cartoonist of the New York *Daily News.* Says Gallo: "I asked him for his list of greatest athletes in each sport and he took out a pen and scribbled these names. He was proud that he knew each of the men named personally."

Boxing—Jack Dempsey
Baseball—Babe Ruth
Football—Bronko Nagurski
Horse Racing—Eddie Arcaro
Basketball—Bill Russell
Bowling—Andy Varipapa
Tennis—Bill Tilden
Golf—Walter Hagen

XIII

The World Of Wheels

Bill Libby's 12 Most-Exciting Indianapolis 500s

Among his 60 books, Billy Libby has written nine on auto racing. He was reared in Indianapolis and the 500 is his favorite sporting event.

1. Foyt's First, 1961—The brilliant Parnelli Jones, his goggles filling with blood after a piece of metal gashed his scalp, led until his engine went bad. Dependable Rodger Ward led until his engine went bad. The fabulous A. J. Foyt, then a hot kid, led until he had to pit for fuel with 25 miles left. Eddie Sachs, who may have wanted to win this race more than any man, suddenly was speeding toward a certain victory until a tire went bad. Instead of gambling on it, he pitted to replace it with 7½ miles left. Foyt won his first 500 by eight seconds. He went on to win four. Sachs never won one and was killed here.
2. DePalma Debacle, 1912—The great Ralph DePalma led by five laps with five laps to go when his engine tore apart. He sputtered along while Joe Dawson passed him again and again. When his engine stopped less than a mile from the finish line, DePalma and his mechanic got out and pushed the car toward home, but Dawson and

A.J. Foyt wins the 1967 Indy 500, one of his record four triumphs in that most celebrated of auto-racing events.

UPI

others kept passing until Dawson won.

3. Shaw Holds On, 1937—After 10 years of trying for his first victory at this hard place, Wilbur Shaw led by almost two minutes with 30 laps left when his engine lost its oil. Figuring out how much he could slow down and still win, Shaw nursed his sick car through the last laps to hold off Ralph Hepburn by 2.16 seconds, closest Indy finish ever.

4. Owner's Choice, 1947—Sliding off the track to avoid a fatal crash by Shorty Cantlon, Bill Holland fell far back, but drove daringly to pull far in front. Veteran teammate Mauri Rose was second in a sister Blue Crown car. Owner Lou Moore gave Holland the "EZ" sign and as he slowed to a conservative run toward seemingly certain victory, Rose made up a minute in the last 100 laps, passed the startled rookie, and won.

5. To the Hungry, 1960—Defending champion Rodger Ward and long-denied Jim Rathmann dueled dangerously through the last 200 miles, passing and repassing one another, until Ward slowed with a worn tire with three laps left and let Rathmann win by less than 13 seconds.
6. No Fourth for Meyer, 1939—In a race in which Floyd Roberts became the first former winner to die at the track, Wilbur Shaw came from a minute back to catch Lou Meyer with 20 miles left. Meyer lost control, skidded and had to pit to replace damaged tires, but Shaw ran out of fuel and had to pit, too. Trying to pass Shaw with three laps left, Meyer lost control and crashed. Shaw won. Both won three here.
7. The Turbo Dies, 1967—Driving Andy Granatelli's controversial STP Turbine car, Parnelli Jones had a huge lead when a ball bearing broke and the engine quit with four laps left. A. J. Foyt flew past for his third triumph.
8. The Turbo Quits Again, 1968—The very next year it was Joe Leonard in the controversial turbocar who was way ahead when a rod broke in the engine with nine laps left. Bobby Unser took his first triumph.
9. No Fourth for Shaw, 1941—On race-day morning, fire destroyed some garages. Wilbur Shaw's car was saved, but fire hoses washed the markings off his spare tires which had been marked as unbalanced, not to be used. Three-time winner Shaw led by 80 seconds with 150 miles to go when the right rear wheel bent, possibly because of an unbalanced tire, sending the car into a crash. Mauri Rose relieved Floyd Davis in 14th place with 320 miles left and steadily moved up to win.
10. No Third for Vuky, 1955—Tough Bill Vukovich might have been going for a fourth straight triumph. In 1952, he led by two miles with 100 miles left when a pivot pin in his steering assembly cracked. Struggling with his steering, he still led until it pulled apart 20 miles from the finish, sending him into the wall, while Troy Ruttman went on to win. In 1953 and 1954, Vuky won. In 1955, he led by a mile when cars crashed in front of

him and he sailed over one, over the wall, to his death. Bob Sweikert went on to win.

11. Cooper Crashes, 1924—At 300 miles, Joe Boyer took over Slim Corum's Duesenberg and began to move up from far back. The great Jimmy Murphy led until he skidded out of it at 350 miles. Boyer took the lead from Earl Cooper at 450 miles. Cooper tried to take it back at 470 miles, but lost control and crashed. Boyer won. Three-time national champ Cooper never won.
12. Foyt Takes Fourth, 1977—Tom Sneva, Bobby Unser and Johnny Rutherford flirted with 200 m.p.h. in time trials, but failed in the race. Gordon Johncock looked like the winner until his engine sputtered to a stop with 16 laps left. Driving conservatively, canny A. J. Foyt sped past to become, finally, the first driver to win this cruel classic a fourth time.

12 Politicos Who Bicycle

1. Former President Jimmy Carter
2. Former President Gerald Ford
3. New York City Mayor Ed Koch
4. Former New York City Mayor John Lindsay
5. Former Senator Jacob Javits, New York
6. Senator Paul Tsongas, Massachusetts
7. Representative Glenn Anderson, California
8. Representative Bob Edgar, Pennsylvania
9. Representative Jim Jones, Oklahoma
10. Representative Ralph Regula, Ohio
11. Representative Bob Eckhardt, Texas
12. Representative Austin Murphy, Pennsylvania

SOURCE: James J. Hayes, Bicycle Manufacturers Association of America, Inc.

Ex-President Carter likes to jog, fish, play softball—and ride a bike.
BMAA/Sports Photo Source

5 Movies in Which the Use of a Bicycle Is Prominent

1. *The Six-Day Bike Rider*
2. *The Bicycle Thief*
3. *Butch Cassidy and the Sundance Kid*
4. *Breaking Away*
5. *A Little Romance*

SOURCE: Philip J. Burke, Bicycle Manufacturers Association of America.

8 Great Bicycle Tours or Routes

1. Tour of the Scioto River (TOSRV)—20th year (1981). Two days (Mother's Day weekend), 210 miles, Columbus, Ohio, to Portsmouth, Ohio, and return.
2. TransAmerica Bicycle Trail—The 4,250-mile trail runs coast-to-coast over back roads from Astoria, Oregon, to Youngstown, Virginia, through 10 states.
3. Pacific Coast Bicentennial Bike Route—A 1,000-mile long route down the California coast.

Joe E. Brown starred in "The Six-Day Bike Rider".

BMAA/Sports Photo Source

4. Register's Annual Great Bicycle Ride Across Iowa (RAGBRAI)—The Des Moines *Register-Tribune* sponsors this event each August with over 5,000 people joining in.
5. East Coast Bicycle Route—A map route over existing roads, from Massachusetts to Virginia. It will be extended north to Maine and south to Florida.

6. New York's Five-Boro Bike Tour—The 1980 event attracted more than 12,000 for a day-long, 40-mile jaunt through the streets of the Big Apple.
7. Mountains to Sea Bike Route—From the Great Smokey Mountains to the Outerbanks, 700-plus miles across North Carolina.
8. Wisconsin Bikeway—Snakes along 300 miles of back country and farm roads between Kenosha and La Crosse.

SOURCE: William C. Wilkinson III, Bicycle Manufacturers Association of America, Inc.

Roller Skating's 34 Greatest American Artistic, Speed, and Hockey Players

The following lists, courtesy of *Skate Magazine,* were suggested by Larry Bortstein, a free-lance writer based in Colorado and the author of numerous books and magazine stories on sports.

BEST AMERICAN MEN ARTISTIC ROLLER SKATERS

1. Cecil Davis, Greeley, Colo.—With partner Phyllis Bulleigh, won the senior pairs national title in 1948, 1949, and 1951. They also won the junior title in 1947 and Davis won the senior singles title in 1949. Davis and Bulleigh introduced the single layback pairs spin.
2. Michael Jacques, Norwood, Mass.—Won an unprecedented seven consecutive senior national titles, from 1966 through 1972. He also won three national pairs titles and three consecutive fours titles.
3. Lex Kane, Pontiac, Mich.—The first to hold an international figure/free title for three consecutive years, 1977, 1978, 1979. He also won singles titles in 1968, figures in 1970 and 1972, pairs in 1969 and two national speed skating titles for good measure.
4. John Matejec, Tulsa, Okla.—After winning the juvenile figure/free title in 1948, John came back four years later to win the gold in singles, pairs and fours competition, all at the National Championships of 1952. At the 1953 championships, he won figures, singles and fours and,

in 1955, he won the senior national figure title.

5. Rick Mullican, Long Beach, Calif.—After winning his first national pairs title in 1955, he came back in 1956 to repeat the victory, but added the national singles title as well. He repeated his singles win in 1957 and 1958 and in his 1958 skating routine, he introduced the traveling camel.
6. J. W. Norcross, Jr., Greeley, Colo.—The only skater ever to win senior national titles in figures, singles, pairs and fours all in the same year, 1950. In 1947 and 1948, Norcross had also won consecutive senior titles in figure/free skating.
7. Ron Robovitsky, Detroit, Mich.—With his sister, Gail, he won 10 national pairs titles, including six consecutive senior pairs titles, from 1967-72. The Robovitsky team also won the World Championship three times, and pioneered double extension, one hand lifts, and the traveling camel impossible.
8. Dave Tassinari, Norwood, Mass.—Pioneered free dance with Patricia Fogerty, winning national titles in 1964, 1965 and 1966. Also won senior pairs titles in 1963, 1964 and 1965 with partner Diana Kearn. This pairs team was the first to perform the jump outer back camel. Tassinari also won four titles in 1961, 1962, 1965, and 1966.
9. Adolph Wacker, Akron, Ohio—Won the senior dance national championship with partner Linda Mottice seven consecutive times, from 1962-68. It's a record that's never been equaled.
10. Edgar Watrous, New Britain, Conn.—This winner of the senior singles title in 1955 and 1956 skated the senior national finals for 10 out of 11 years, regaining his title in 1965. The one year he missed was due to an injury.

BEST AMERICAN WOMEN ARTISTIC ROLLER SKATERS

1. April Allen, Houston, Tex.—Greatly influenced all competition to follow her with an outstanding dance quality on skates. Won individual titles for four consecutive years, 1969-72, as well as pairs titles in 1965, 1967, and 1973.

2. Laurene Anselmi, Pontiac, Mich.—Never defeated in singles competition. Won a total of 17 national titles, including the senior title four straight years. Laurene also won one speed skating title and several figure skating titles. Her career went from 1947 through 1954.
3. Fleurette Arseneault, East Meadow, N.Y.—A three-time world dance champion and Pan-American gold medalist with partner Dan Littel. The duo also won three consecutive international dance titles in 1977, 1978, 1979, the same years they won worlds. Fleurette also won junior international dance title in 1972, free dance in 1975, dance in 1974, and a figure skating title in 1972.
4. Phyllis Bulleigh, Greeley, Colo.—With partner Cecil Davis, won senior pairs national title in 1948, 1949 and 1951. They also had won the junior title in 1947 and Phyllis won the figure/free skating title in her division in 1948 as well. Cecil and Phyllis introduced the single layback pairs spin.
5. Natalie Dunn, Bakersfield, Calif.—Three-time world champion (1976, 1977, 1978) and Pan American gold medalist in 1979. Natalie was the first woman to clean a triple revolution jump at nationals, and was senior national champ in 1973 and 1974, winning junior titles in singles and pairs in 1972.
6. Darlene Edwards, Columbus, Ohio—Championship titles that span a decade from 1967 to her 1976 world pairs title, with partner Ron Sabo. In singles, she won titles in 1959, 1960, 1961, and 1964, in addition to her 1956 Diaper Division win. Won national pairs title in 1974 with Mark Revere and won again in 1975 and 1976 with Sabo. The 1976 world title was their second, having won in 1975.
7. Charlotte Ludwig, Elizabeth, N.J.—Won senior pairs title in 1946 with partner Frank Salvage, skating in what was then a separate confederation from USACRS (United States Amateur Confederation of Roller Skating). Repeated her win with partner Jude Cull in 1947 and 1948 and won singles in 1948. Won senior pairs title again in 1950 and 1951, again with Cull.

Natalie Dunn was the Pan American Games gold medalist for artistic roller skating in 1979.

Skate Magazine/Sports Photo Source

8. Linda Mottice, Akron, Ohio—Won the senior dance national championship with partner Adolph Wacker seven consecutive times, from 1962-1968. It's a record that has never been equaled.
9. Jane Puracchio, East Meadow, N.Y.—Won fours title in 1965, pairs and dance in 1966, pairs in 1967, dance in 1970. She won three titles in 1971: figures, dance, and free dance. Then won the national senior international dance title with James Stephens in 1973 and, in 1974, this team won both nationals and worlds. Jane then teamed with Kerry Cavazzi for two more senior international titles in 1975 and 1976, and the Cavazzi/Puracchio team won worlds both those years.
10. Gail Robovitsky, Detroit, Mich.—With her brother, Ron, she won 10 national pairs titles, including six consecutive senior pairs titles from 1967-72. On her own, Gail also won singles titles in 1967 and 1968. The Robovitsky team won the world championship three times and pioneered double extensions, one hand lifts, and the traveling camel impossible.

GREATEST AMERICAN MEN SPEED ROLLER SKATERS

1. Pat Bergin, Irving, Tex.—Winner of 16 national titles and one of the great speed skaters of the 60s. Pat won his first title in 1958, then won every national individual title from 1965 to 1972, an eight-year string. Pat also won relay titles with his teammates in 1966, 1968, 1969, 1971, and 1972 with double wins in 1969 and 1971.
2. Roland Cioni, New York, N.Y.—Held the World Professional speed skating title from 1914, when he was 15, until his retirement from competition in 1954.
3. George Grudza, Penndal, Pa.—A record-setter with the start, passing ability and endurance to win the national junior title in 1957 and 1958, then the Senior title in 1960 and 1964.
4. Scott Harrity, Pontiac, Mich.—Beginning in the youngest division of racing, Scott won the national title from 1960 through 1965. He also excelled in artistic

Tim Small has won 19 national speed roller skating titles.
Skate Magazine/Sports Photo Source

skating, being the youngest national competitor to clean a double axle in 1964.

5. Tony Merilli, St. Louis, Mo.—One of the great competitors with an outstanding start and great passing ability. Won the senior national title in 1942 and 1944.
6. Eddie Perales, Torrance, Calif.—A late bloomer who competed in the younger divisions without great success, then decided to practice. He practiced so hard that no one could beat him. He won the senior national title in 1961, 1962, and 1963, the first time a senior skater had held a title for three consecutive years.
7. Tim Small, Miami, Fla.—Holds the record for most national titles—19. In relays with teammates, he won titles in 1968, then every year from 1972 through 1976, often with two or three different relay titles in one year. In individual races, titles came every year from 1971 through 1976. For two consecutive years, 1975 and 1976, he won every event he could enter for a clean sweep of all the senior national titles.
8. Harold Wyant, Dayton, Ohio—Set speed skating records that stood for years as he won the senior national title two years in a row, 1946 and 1947.

GREATEST AMERICAN WOMEN SPEED ROLLER SKATERS

1. Pamela Dickey, Pasadena, Tex.—Undefeated in national competition from 1959 through 1964, a string of six consecutive titles. Pamela also won relay titles in 1963 and 1964.
2. Susie Johnson, Irving, Tex.—Held national titles from 1965 through 1970, another string of six consecutive titles. In addition to her 1967 individual title, she and her teammates also won two relays, and she was on winning relay teams again in 1971 and 1972 for a career total of 10 national titles.
3. Jamie London, Irving, Tex.—Undefeated in national competition from 1967 through 1972, tying Pamela Dickey's record for consecutive titles. Jamie also won the freshman relay title with her teammates in 1972.

4. Mary Merrell, Santa Ana, Ca.—All time record holder for senior individual titles in 1959, 1960, 1961, 1963, 1966, and 1967, and two relay titles in 1967 and 1970. Mary also placed second at nationals in the senior two-lady relay with her daughter Diane in 1975—so far the only mother-daughter team to place at nationals. (Diane won the junior title that year.)
5. Evelyn Olsen, Oakland, Ca.—Won the senior title in 1950, 1952, 1954, and 1955, the first to win four titles in the senior national championships.
6. Marcia Yager, Loveland, Ohio—The first senior skater since Mary Merrell to win three consecutive national titles, in 1975, 1976, and 1977. She also won younger division titles in 1972 and 1973 and relay titles in 1972, 1973 and 1975. In 1976, in addition to her individual title, she was on the winning team in all four senior relay events, giving her five national titles in a single year.

GREATEST AMERICAN ROLLER HOCKEY STARS

Note: In countries such as Argentina, Brazil, Portugal, and Spain, roller hockey's attraction as a spectator sport is second only to soccer. Roller hockey players in the United States have yet to achieve such recognition, but they keep skating, playing a game that's faster, more fascinating and less violent than its counterpart on ice. National championships are held every two years.

1. Johnny "Preacher" Black, Lubbock, Tex.—Founded a hockey league with his brother Henry in 1949; founded the winningest team in American roller hockey, the Rolling Ghosts, and played on the 1966 World Team.
2. Dickie Chado, Glendora, Ca.—Aggressive young player chosen for World Team in 1974, 1976, and 1980; played on national championship winner in 1974.
3. Pat Ferguson, Cumberland, Md.—Led team to national championships in 1973, 1975, and 1980, and the National Sports Festival title in 1979. World team player in 1974, 1978 and 1980.
4. Dub Graham, Port Neches, Tex.—Goalie for four straight years as his team won the national championship in 1966, 1967, 1968, and 1969. World Team goalie in 1968 and 1970.

5. Roy Huckaby, Port Neches, Tex.—Consistent scoring and quick play made him a World Team player in 1966, 1968, 1970, and 1972, as well as a member of the national championship teams of 1966, 1967, 1968, and 1969.
6. Bill Sisson, Lubbock, Tex.—Began playing with Rolling Ghosts in 1954, helping them win 10 of their 11 national championships—in 1961, 1962, 1963, 1964, 1965, 1970, 1971, 1972, 1976, and 1977. World Team player in 1966 and 1968 and coach of the World Team in 1978 and 1980.
7. David Sisson, Lubbock, Tex.—Goalie for the Rolling Ghosts, the team winning 11 national championships, 1961-65, 1970-72, 1976, 1977, 1979. World Team goalie 1966, 1968, 1972, 1976, and still playing strong.
8. Dickie Sisson, Lubbock, Tex.—Member of the Rolling Ghosts and one of the most aggressive players in the game. A big reason for 11 national championships, a World Team member in 1966, 1968, 1972, and 1976, and, like David, still playing.
9. Dickie Thibodeaux, Port Neches, Tex.—One of the highly skilled players from the national championship team of 1966, 1967, 1968, and 1969, a World Team member in 1966, 1968, 1970, and 1972.
10. Danny Trussell, Albany, Ore.—Outstanding skater and team leader from the Pacific Northwest, a World Team member in 1970 and 1972.

Note: Most of these players are still skating for their team in national competition. Those who are not playing "officially" are active in scrimmage games, practices, coaching and officiating. The average age for these 10 all-stars is 37.

XIV

You Can Look It Up

Maury White's 10 Favorite Incredibly Tough Sports Quiz Questions

Maury White, sports columnist for the Des Moines *Register,* is by his own description "a fourth-generation newspaper guy in Iowa. My great granddad started a weekly at Emmetsburg, Iowa, in 1869 and since then at least one of every generation has been so engaged. I grew up in a succession of back shops as a printer's devil. A couple of weeks after I graduated from high school and not long after I turned 17, my father died. My mother and I took over the Manila *Times,* a weekly. That's when I started writing a column, and everything else in the paper except the locals.

"I went to work for the *Register* in 1946. Been there ever since. I started writing columns in fairly short order, then became a lead columnist in March, 1965, when Sec Taylor finally cashed it in at age 78 or so. I am currently employed in the same capacity, much older, little wiser and still semi-impoverished."

1. Who is the only basketball coach to have a career losing record at Kansas University?
2. What official PGA tour tournament not only never has had a champion repeat, but has never had a champion even try to defend his title?

3. Once, and only once, a major league team and all its players had the same batting averages after a game as before. Elucidate, please.
4. What month in what year produced the three greatest sports figures?
5. A pro football player, please, who played on three different teams in three different leagues in the same city?
6. What player scored the highest percentage of his team's points in a major league professional basketball game?
7. Name me a player who has started on both offense and defense in Super Bowl action?
8. Quick now, the shortest known field goal in college football history?
9. The late Phog Allen, longtime coach at Kansas U. and a few other places, had many pupils who went on to fame. The one surest of being mentioned in history books in 100 years is?
10. Name the only NFL player who has truly tasted both the best and worst of it for an entire season?

Answers

6. In November 1954, George Mikan scored 15 of the loser's points (or 84 percent) as the Fort Wayne Pistons beat the Minneapolis Lakers, 19-18.
7. E. J. Holub was a starting linebacker for the Kansas City Chiefs in Super Bowl I and the center in Super Bowl IV.
8. Paul Marchese of Kent State kicked a 16-yarder in 1977. Since that counts 10 yards of end zone and the ball was not quite to the goal line, Marchese set up less than six yards behind scrimmage, about as close as humanly possible.
9. While some may opt for Adolph Rupp, Clyde Lovellette, etc., my choice is Bess Truman, who once lived in the White House with President Harry S Truman. Allen coached her high school team.
10. Larry Ball played with a Miami Dolphin team that won every game in 1972 and a Tampa Bay team that lost 'em all in 1977.

1. Dr. James Naismith, inventor of the game of basketball, went 55-60 as Jayhawk coach for nine seasons, the first in 1898. Every other coach has been .571 or better.
2. The winner of the Tallahassee Open, annually played opposite the Tournament of Champions for players not qualified for the T of C, gets a berth in the T of C (where the loot and prestige is much greater) the following year.
3. The 1940 Chicago White Sox were victims of Bob Feller's no-hitter on opening day. Players and team were batting .000 before and after.
4. I will settle for February 1895, which brought us George Halas, George Gipp, and Babe Ruth.
5. Placekicker Ben Agajanian was with the All-America Conference Dons, 1947-48; NFL Rams, 1953; and AFL Chargers (now San Diego), 1960, when all represented Los Angeles.

John Duxbury's 15 Toughest Basketball Questions

A St. Louis newspaperman, John Duxbury answers questions in *The Sporting News.*

1. When Wilt Chamberlain scored 100 points for the Philadelphia Warriors against New York on March 2, 1962, who led the Knicks in scoring?
2. Who was the coach of the only team to beat an Adolph Rupp-coached Kentucky team in an NCAA championship game?
3. Who led the Boston Celtics in rebounding the season before Bill Russell joined them?
4. Who was the regular center on John Wooden's first NCAA championship team at UCLA (1964)?
5. Who was the first player to score 20 or more points in an NCAA championship game?

6. Who was the first forward to average more than 30 points a game in an NBA season?
7. When CCNY beat Bradley, 71-68, in the 1950 NCAA title game to become the first team to win the NCAA and NIT in the same season, who was the leading scorer in the game?
8. Who was the leading scorer for the 1948 gold-medal-winning U.S. Olympic team?
9. Who was the Most Valuable Player in the first National Invitation Tournament?
10. Who is the only major college player other than Frank Selvy and Pete Maravich to average more than 40 points a game in a season?
11. How many NBA championship teams did Red Auerbach coach that didn't include Bill Russell as a member of the team?
12. What member of the Philadelphia Warriors won the NBA scoring title in 1952-53, 1953-54 and 1954-55?
13. Who was the only player on the 1955-56 Philadelphia NBA championship team who had no college experience?
14. Who are the two Olympic high jumpers who played in the NBA?
15. Basketball Hall of Famer George Mikan had a brother who also played in the NBA. What was his first name?

Answers

7. Gene Melchiorre of Bradley with 16 points.
8. Alex Groza of Kentucky, 78 points in seven games.
9. Don Shields of Temple
10. Johnny Neumann of Mississippi, 40.1 in 1970-71.
11. None
12. Neil Johnston
13. Joe Graboski
14. Dwight (Dike) Eddleman of Illinois and Walter (Buddy) Davis of Texas A&M.
15. Ed

1. Richie Guerin with 39 points.
2. Don Haskins of Texas Western in 1966.
3. Jack Nichols, 625 in 1955-56.
4. Fred Slaughter
5. Washington State guard Kirk Gebert, who scored 21 points in a 39-34 loss to Wisconsin in 1941.
6. Jack Twyman of Cincinnati, 31.2 in 1959-60.

Pete Enich's 24 Sports Trivia Questions Every Trivia Player Should Know

The self-proclaimed champion sports trivia expert of Kansas City (Kansas and Missouri), Pete Enich is a former all-state high school quarterback, all-state high school basketball player, former sports information director of Kansas U. and currently public safety information officer for Kansas City.

"You have to start young to be good at sports trivia," Enich says. "When I was eight years old, I read my first copy of *The Sporting News.* I still have a copy of every issue printed since then, almost every issue of *Sports Illustrated* and Street & Smith's basketball and football yearbooks. I can be stumped on one question, but over a period of an hour, I wear a man down."

1. Who was Packey East?
2. Babe Ruth hit one minor league home run. In what city?
3. Who hit the first tee shot in Masters history?
4. In 1904 this St. Louis Cardinal pitcher achieved an amazing record for complete games. He started 39 contests for the Redbirds and completed every one of them. Who was he?
5. What was the first track and field world record set in the morning?
6. What former University of Missouri athlete once struck out Babe Ruth 10 times in a row and 19 out of 31 at-bats?
7. Who is Jennifer Edwards and why were NFL fans saying those terrible things about her?
8. What was so unusual about the 1941 National Football League draft?
9. What former major league baseball figure was the co-owner of the film rights to *Gone With the Wind?*

Jack Dempsey, left, squares off for a 1951 television exhibition with Packey East.
UPI

10. If a high jumper clears 7 feet, 2 ½ inches, how fast will he be going when he hits the pit?
11. Who was the timekeeper for the famous Dempsey-Tunney long-count fight?
12. Who was the first football player from an all-black college to play in the now-defunct All-Star Game?
13. How did the 1970 Pittsburgh pitching staff compare to a butcher shop?
14. Only one man in history made first team All-America in football at two Big Ten schools. Name him.
15. Who was the first rookie to lead the National League in home runs?
16. Who was the first man to qualify for the Indy 500 at a speed in excess of 100 m.p.h.?

17. Rocky Marciano won all 49 of his fights, 43 by KO. Only five fighters went the distance with him. One man went 10 rounds against Marciano twice. Name him.
18. Who was the first woman to run a five-minute mile?
19. One of five UCLA players named to the first U.S. Olympic basketball team, this Helms Foundation Hall of Famer played the role of Dr. Frankenstein in the classic horror film. Who was he?
20. Who was the first baseball player to use a glove?
21. Who is the only woman to have her name inscribed on the Stanley Cup?
22. The first run ever scored against the hapless New York Mets came in a most appropriate fashion. Explain.
23. Who was the first lineman to be selected as the first choice in an NFL player draft?
24. The story of Johnny Unitas' rise from sandlot football to the NFL is now legendary. He played for the semi-pro Bloomfield Rams in 1955 before leading the Baltimore Colts to world championships in 1958 and 1959. What former major league pitcher did Unitas beat out at the quarterback position for the minor league Rams in 1955?

Answers

Southern California for the first half-century.

20. Charles C. Waite, first baseman for the National Association's Boston Club, in 1875.
21. Marguerite Norris Riker, president of the Detroit Red Wings' two Stanley Cup championship teams in 1952 and 1955.
22. The Mets' first regular-season game was on April 11, 1962, against the St. Louis Cardinals. Pitcher Roger Craig committed a balk in the first inning, allowing Bill White to score from third, opening the door for a season of errors, miscues, tragi-comedy, and 120 defeats.
23. Ki Aldrich, center, Texas Christian, picked by the Chicago Cardinals in 1939.
24. Ed Rakow, former hurler for the Dodgers, A's, Tigers, and Braves.

1. Bob Hope's *nom de plume* as an amateur boxer in Cleveland.
2. Toronto, Canada.
3. Ralph Stonehouse, 10 A.M., March 22, 1934.
4. John Taylor (20-19 record).
5. Shot put, 58 feet, ¼ inch, Chuck Fonville, Kansas University Relays, April 17, 1948, 9:46 a.m.
6. Hubert (Shucks) Pruett, St. Louis Browns, 1922-24, who had a career record of 29-48.
7. Jennifer played the lead role of Heidi in the November 17, 1968, NBC dramatization of the Swiss mountain girl from the story books. The New York Jets played the Oakland Raiders the same day and the exciting ending of the game was taken off the air to allow for the start of the film.
8. In 1941 the Chicago Bears defended their world championship by beating the New York Giants, 37-9, at Wrigley Field before the smallest crowd ever for a championship game (13,341). George Halas entertained the NFL owners in the Palmer House that evening and during dinner they held the annual college draft. It took just under three hours.
9. New York Mets owner Joan Whitney Payson who, along with her brother, Jock Whitney, owned the 1939 film classic.
10. 14.5 m.p.h.
11. Paul Beeler.
12. Johnny Sample, Maryland State.
13. Three of the Pirate hurlers that year were (Bob) Moose, (Bob) Veale and (John) Lamb.
14. Alex Agase, guard, Illinois (1942) and Purdue (1943).
15. Harry Lumley of Brooklyn, who hit nine in 1904.
16. Rene Thomas of France won the pole position for the 1919 500 with an average qualifying speed of 104.70 m.p.h.
17. Ted Lowry.
18. Diane Leather of Birmingham, England
19. Frank Lubin, named by Helms as the greatest player in

XV

Swifter, Higher, Stronger

Stan Saplin's All-Time Track Team of Smiths

A former sportswriter (for the New York *Journal-American*) and publicist (New York University, the New York Rangers), Stan Saplin calls his favorite sport track and field. He has covered several Olympic Games, contributed articles on track for magazines and books, and served as public address announcer for meets at Madison Square Garden. He was a track commentator for CBS and NBC and has written about track for the *Encyclopedia Brittanica* and the Menke *Encyclopedia of Sports.*

SPRINTS

Dean Smith, 1952 U.S. 100-meter champion; member, 1952 Olympic champion 400-meter relay team.

Ronnie Ray Smith, equaled world 100-meter record, 1968; member 1968 Olympic champion 400-meter relay team.

Tommie Smith, 1968 Olympic 200-meter champion; broke world 200-meter record, 1966; broke world 400-meter record, 1967.

Sprinter Tommie Smith, center, raises fist to highlight racial tension in the world after winning the 200-meter gold medal at the 1968 Olympic Games in Mexico City. He's joined in protest by John Carlos, who finished third.

UPI

John Smith, 1970 and 1971 U.S. 440-yard champion; broke world 440-yard record, 1971.

Willie Smith, 1979 and 1980 U.S. 400-meter champion.

MIDDLE DISTANCES

Bill Smith, 1881 U.S. 880-yard champion.

T.H. Smith, 1878 U.S. one-mile champion.

DISTANCE

Tracy Smith, 1966 U.S. 10,000-meter champion; 1967 and 1973 U.S. indoor 3-mile champion.
Bernard Joseph Smith, 1941 U.S. marathon champion.

HURDLES

Forrest Smithson*, 1908 Olympic 110-meter champion; broke world record, 120-yard and 110-meter, 1908.
Walker Smith, 1919 and 1920 U.S. indoor 60-yard champion.
J. Walter Smith, 1942 U.S. 400-meter champion.

STEEPLECHASE

Randy Smith, 1975 and 1976 U.S. champion.

HIGH JUMP

Willard Smith, 1944 U.S. champion.

POLE VAULT

Harry Smith, 1925 U.S. champion.
Guinn Smith, 1948 Olympic champion.
Steve Smith, 1973 indoor champion; broke world indoor record, 1973.

LONG JUMP

Theodore Smith, 1933 U.S. indoor champion.

TRIPLE JUMP

Dave Smith, 1971 U.S. indoor champion.

* How'd he get in there?

Herman L. Masin's 21 Former Members of the All-America High School Track Team Who Made a Giant Leap Forward upon Other Fields, on Other Days

Herman L. Masin is the celebrated editor of *Scholastic Coach* magazine, the bible of high school sports.

	ATHLETE	YEAR	EVENT	OTHER FIELD
1.	Roosevelt Grier, Roselle, N.J.	1951	Shotput, javelin	Pro football, show business
2.	Charlie Powell, San Diego, Ca.	1951	Shotput	Boxing
3.	Joe Childress, Odessa, Tex.	1952	Dashes	Football
4.	Gene Orowitz*, Collingswood, N.J.	1954	Javelin	Television
5.	Billy Cannon, Baton Rouge, La.	1955	Dash	Football
6.	Mike McKeever, Los Angeles, Ca.	1957	Shotput	Football
7.	Willie Davis, Los Angeles, Ca.	1958	Long jump	Baseball
8.	Mel Renfro, Portland, Ore.	1959	High hurdles	Football
9.	Paul Warfield, Warren, Ohio	1960	Low hurdles	Football
10.	Gale Sayers, Omaha, Neb.	1961	Long jump	Football
11.	Elvin Bethea, Trenton, N.J.	1964	Shotput	Football
12.	Bobby Bonds, Riverside, Ca.	1965	Long jump	Baseball
13.	Willie Crawford, Los Angeles, Ca.	1965	Long jump	Baseball
14.	Terry Bradshaw, Shreveport, La.	1966	Javelin	Football
15.	Mel Gray, Santa Rosa, Ca.	1967	Long jump	Football
16.	Isaac Curtis, Santa Ana, Ca.	1968	Low hurdles	Football
17.	Sam Cunningham, Santa Barbara, Ca.	1969	Shotput	Football
18.	Lynn Swann, San Mateo, Ca.	1970	Long jump	Football
19.	Russ Francis, Pleasant Hill, Ore.	1971	Javelin	Football
20.	Lonnie Shelton, Bakersfield, Ca.	1973	Discus	Basketball
21.	Charles White, San Fernando, Ca.	1976	Int. hurdles	Football

* Adds Masin: "So what is anyone with a name like Gene Orowitz doing up there with the immortals? And you never heard of him in television? Well, just knock on the door of the 'Little House on the Prairie' and ask for Gene Orowitz. Michael Landon will immediately step forward. Back at good old Collingswood (N.J.) High in 1954, Gene (Michael Landon) Orowitz was the greatest javelin thrower in the country, with a best mark of 193'4".

"You could make a helluva football team out of these high school track immortals. Receivers—Lynn Swann and Paul Warfield; tackles—Elvin Bethea and Rosie Grier; tight ends—Russ Francis and Mike McKeever; halfbacks—Gale Sayers and Billy Cannon; fullback —Sam Cunningham; quarterback—Who else? And if we needed a center, we'd ask Lonnie Shelton to give it a try. We'd keep Charlie Powell around for when the fight started, and plant Gene Orowitz in front of the locker room to distract the women reporters."

Elliott Denman's 12 Greatest American Walkers

In 1956, Elliott Denman walked from the Bronx to Australia by way of New York University's Ohio Field, the U.S. Olympic trials in Baltimore, and an Air Force jet. Down under, he came up with an 11th place in the 50-kilometer walk at the Melbourne Olympics and has been a walking activist ever since. He indulges in the pastime for competitive and recreational reasons but, as a sportswriter for the Asbury Park (N.J.) *Press* for 17 years, has never taken a pedestrian approach to athletic journalism.

1. Meriwether Lewis and William Clark (one and inseparable).
2. Larry Young
3. Henry Laskau
4. Harry S. Truman
5. Ronald Zinn
6. Edward Payson Weston
7. Abraham Lincoln Monteverde
8. Ronald O. Laird
9. Todd Scully
10. Rudy Haluza
11. Marco Evoniuk
12. Carl Schueler

Vincent Reel's "138 Women Track and Field Stars with Names I Like"

S. F. Vincent Reel, track coach at the University of Redlands, is also editor of *Women's Track World* magazine. One of the most popular features in the magazine is the Kaleidoscope column which has included "names I like" in each issue. Every name on this list came from a legitimate result sheet or newspaper report or track program, according to Reel, who says, "Honestly, we didn't make any of them up."

1. Gay Munday
2. Chee Swee Lee
3. Princy Balthasar
4. Crickett Cupid
5. Sandy Beach
6. Melody Lavender

7,8,9. China, Fehe and Nneondi Aroh

10. Anna Trotter
11. Primrose Abilla
12. Kapitolina Lotova
13. Tweety Wolf

71. Terri Christmas
72. Debbie Boomsema
73. Cornbread Johnson
74. Terkaler Shegog
75. Luigina Torso
76. Sue Poteats
77. Cindy Beanblossom
78. Sandy Mustard
79. Dawn Day
80. Sally Shoots
81. Betta Little
82. Rocky Racette

14. Beverly Hill
15. Xiehle Baldwin
16. Skyler Ousley
17. CoCo de Arakal
18. Mar Mar Min
19. Tiffany Choy
20. Nu Nu Yee
21. Tin Tin Ohu
22. Sue New
23. Pauline Vakamootoo
24. Ouch Lay
25. Hava Shakhar
26. Lee In Sook
27,28,29. Sylvia, Alice and Caroline Dingwell
30. Zizi Fritz
31. Rhonda Zapp
32. Zsa-Zsa Yow
33. Marjorie Kaput
34. Winsome Langley
35. Zeppi Long
36. Susi Ruhl
37. Gail Wigle
38. Princess Lindsey
39. Thin Proch
40. Inchin Ham
41. Susan Stoops
42. Betsy Clogg
43. April Hickey
44. Tangye Wallace
45. Radius Guess
46. Willijena Oggs
47. Leyda Fidalgo
48. Missy Guhl
49. Sue Long
50. Calla Huddle
51. Sharon Wigglesworth
52. Katie Cakebread
53. Anthi Papachristopulous
54. Hindy Bear
55. Fatima Pinto
56. Kusum Chatwal
57. Dee Dee Eddy
58. Fawzi Ali
59. Patty Pink
60. Pam Happy
61. Snoozie Weber
62. Peka Twitchell
63. Sara Ripps
83. Steff Pinskey
84. Sandy Grove
85. Kitty Ho
86. Starlet
87. Peach Payne
88. Beets Kolarik
89. Radious Jacobs
90. Shu Quereshi
91. Sue Slutz
92. Lori Hooker
93. Early Douglas
94. Moo Thorpe
95. Kathy Kuchta
96. Dawna Rose
97. Jennifer Perdue
98. Libby Bell
99. Thea Typhoon
100. Ingrid Sprint
101. Shirley Strong
102. Delight Chambers
103. Twalla Pugh
104. Cici Hopp
105. Krystal Sheets
106. Patty Gaddy
107. Lena Spoof
108. Gigi Goochey
109. Jeneai Cabbage
110. Nwe Nwe Yee
111. Jenifer Tin Lay
112. Connie Kidder
113. Lou Lemmons
114. Jada Yeast
115. Meme Large
116. Sunday Wallen
117. Stormi Guntsch
118. Muffin Miller
119. Sarah Peapple
120. Cximare Adams
121. Be Alt
122. Patti Bean
123. Lucinda Sparrow
124. Carol Ouchi
125. Anne Okey
126. Dawn Braun
127. Cat Watten
128. Bernee Long
129. Nina Redcherries
130. Fita Lovin
131. Busbong Yimploy

64. Zsa Zsa Ziegler
65. Janet Walkup
66. Merri Furlong
67. Karla Amble
68. Linda Griggers
69. Candy Acres
70. Shiavohonne Shy

132. Pranee Kitipongitaya
133. Barbara Inkpen
134. Easter Gabriel
135. Ann Van
136. Renita Dingle
137. Hopey Caudill
138. Schuywana Davis

Giorgio Chinaglia exults over the New York Cosmos' winning of the 1980 Soccer Bowl in Washington.

Wide World

XVI

A Boot In The Grass

Giorgio Chinaglia's 5 Most Memorable Goals

1. Lazio (Rome) vs. Milan, 1969—"My first goal for Lazio. We won, 1-0."
2. Italy vs. Bulgaria, 1972—"We were losing when I came in as a substitute in the second half. Within 30 seconds I had scored and we ended up tying them, 1-1."
3. Lazio vs. Foggia, 1974—"There were just five minutes left and the game was tied. I scored, we won the game, 1-0, and with it the Italian title."
4. Cosmos vs. Seattle, 1977 Soccer Bowl—"With the score tied, 1-1, and six minutes left, I headed one in and we went on to win, 2-1."
5. Cosmos vs. California, 1980—"The one that broke the record (most regular-season career goals in the NASL, 102). Thank God it wasn't a cheap goal, like from a penalty. It was clean."

SOURCE: *Inside Sports.*

Jerry Trecker's 7 Soccer Dreams

Jerry Trecker is a Connecticut school teacher/sports writer who has chased international soccer knowledge for over 25 years. He still thinks the game is special, but with a typically American attitude, thinks it can be made even better.

1. An end to free substitution in American college and high school play—so that our growing number of players will experience the game in its world condition, 90 minutes of effort, pacing, and work. Now, a college or high school player can rest on the bench instead of learning how to handle the pressure of fatigue in the course of the match. Does that make a difference in our players' development? Does Texas have a Lone Star flag?

2. No more mini games—that North American League invention to decide playoff winners. C'mon, fellows, it's time that the league accepted two-game, total-goal series, forgot about its shoot-out in post-season play and let the goal scorers determine the issue.

3. A limit on foreign players, not a quota on North Americans—so that the major professional circuit in the United States and Canada will finally provide a real home for the emerging talents over on our side of the Atlantic. Most nations restrict the number of foreigners, we say there must be a few (three in 1980) North Americans. Somehow, I think we've got the concept backwards for the '80s, even if it was right for the '70s.

4. Soccer games on television without commercials—or at least with the commercials slotted before, during half-

time or after the game. I've never yet seen an opera interrupted, a symphony bisected, a political acceptance speech short-circuited in order to sell a product. Sorry, but I just can't enjoy a continuous action game presented with continuous interruptions. Apparently, not many other people do either.

5. A regular schedule of home games for the United States —which is so regular about making "tours" but so rarely plays anybody in front of the home folks. Until the American fan can expect to see his national team in action at least four or five times a year, how can real interest be built in the international game? At least four matches, one in each region of the land, are a must.

6. The development of reserve teams, indoor and out— so that the home town always has a game to see whenever the soccer weekend has the main club on the road. Until the pros do invest in reserve sides and play a full reserve schedule, they'll continue to be dependent on overseas and limited college resources for the production of top quality talent. It will be costly, but probably must happen. After all, where would baseball be without its minor leagues?

7. A universal indoor code of rules—which could lead to international indoor play. It may not be soccer in its purest form, but the indoor game is exciting, has captured an American audience. It's a place where we can lead instead of follow, an exciting prospect for this decade and the next.

Richard A. Altomare's 10 Best Indoor Soccer Players

Richard A. Altomare is vice president and general manager of the New York Arrows, 1979, 1980 and 1981 champions of the Major Indoor Soccer League.

1. Steve Zungul
2. Fed Grgurev
3. Kai Haaskivi
4. Branko Segota
5. Pat Ercoli
6. Keith Van Eron
7. Shep Messing
8. Mick Poole
9. Alan Mayer
10. Juli Veee

XVII

Clowning and Juggling

Gene Jones' 19 Greatest Jugglers of the Century

Gene Stanley Jones is President of the International Jugglers Association, whose membership numbers more than 1,300, a number of them collegians. Jones has toured internationally as a juggler and variety entertainer under the name of "Geno." With help from I.J.A. historian Dennis Soldati, Jones has developed his lists, which are alphabetical.

MEN

1. Francis Brunn*
2. Rudy Cardenas*
3. Paul Cinquevalli
4. W. C. Fields
5. Dick Franco*
6. Rudy Horn
7. Sergei Ignatov*
8. Kara
9. Bella Kremo
10. Kris Kremo*
11. Bobby May
12. Howard Nickols
13. Enrico Rastelli
14. Salerno

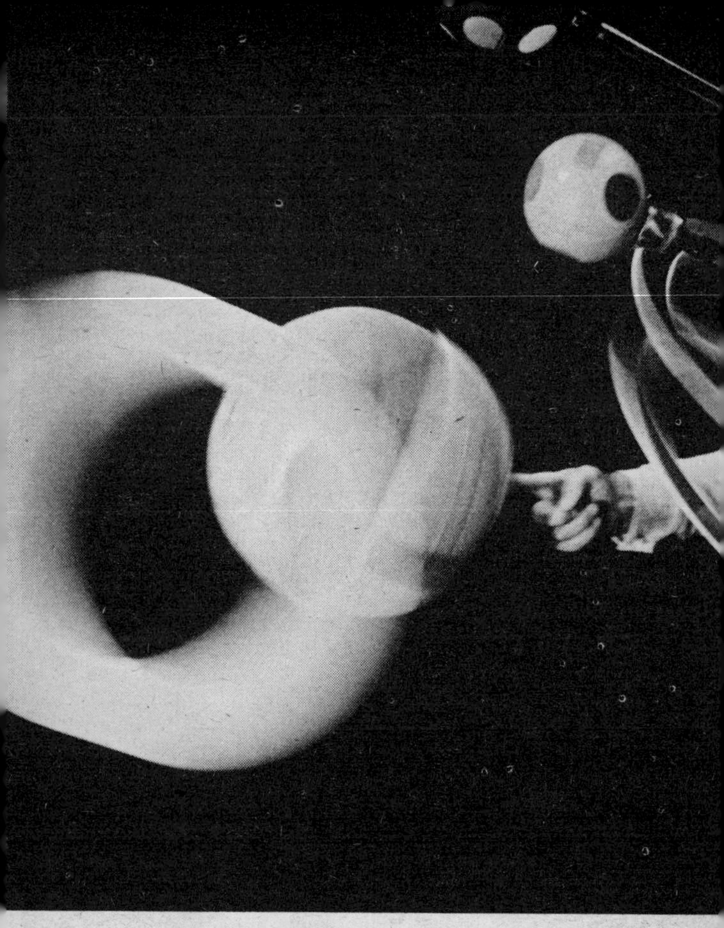

Francis Brunn's juggling feats have brought him fame the world over.
Max Roth/Sports Photo Source

WOMEN

1. Selma Braatz
2. Lottie Brunn*
3. Jenny Jaager
4. Trixie
5. Eva Vida*

* Still actively performing.

Bernie Lincicome's 10 Flakiest Athletes of All Time

Bernie Lincicome is sports editor and columnist of the Ft. Lauderdale *News.*

1. Dizzy Dean
2. Bobby Riggs
3. Tim Rossovich
4. Sparky Lyle
5. Derek Sanderson
6. Ilie Nastase
7. Joe Don Looney
8. Lee Trevino
9. Jimmy Piersall
10. Bill Lee

Dizzy Dean, right, and brother Daffy ham it up in 1935 at the Cardinals' spring training camp in Bradenton, Florida.

UPI

5 More Yogi Berra-isms

1. Billy Martin was distraught. He had locked his keys in his car one day during spring training and he had no idea how to get them out, until his pal, Yogi Berra, came up with the solution. "You gotta call a blacksmith," said Yogi.
2. An admirer noticed Berra wearing a different sweater each night during spring training and asked if Yogi had one in all colors. "The only color I don't have," Berra replied, "is navy brown."
3. A member of the Yankee traveling party entered the lobby of a Chicago hotel and, spotting Berra, jokingly said he was expecting Bo Derek to arrive at 11. "Well," said Berra, "I haven't seen him."
4. A friend told Berra he wanted to go to a particular Fort Lauderdale restaurant, but feared it would be too crowded. "Then why did you wait so long to go now?" Berra asked.
5. At a Yankee party, Berra was asked why he wasn't dancing. "Because," he said, "I got rubber shoes on."

Bob Wolf's 13 Favorite Johnny Logan-isms

Bob Wolf covered the Milwaukee Braves for the Milwaukee *Journal* when the team moved to his city from Boston in 1953. It was an exciting assignment, covering such greats as Henry Aaron, Warren Spahn, and Eddie Mathews, and with the Braves winning two championships. But Wolf got more than he bargained for with the colorful language of Johnny Logan, the team's outstanding shortstop.

1. When told that something he had complained about in the *Journal* was a typographical error: "The hell it was. It was a clean base hit."
2. Upon receiving an award: "I will perish this trophy forever."
3. After seeing "Macbeth" on television: "They've got a new Shakespearean play, 'McBride.' It's got a lot of suspension."

4. Asked to pick the No. 1 baseball player of all time: "I'd have to go with the immoral Babe Ruth."
5. In a speech at a dinner for Stan Musial: "Tonight we're honoring one of the all-time greats of baseball. Stan Musial. He's immoral."
6. To Mrs. Lou Perini aboard the late clubowner's yacht: "You have a very homely yacht."
7. When told about a trade: "Yeah, did you see it on the radio?"
8. Upon being introduced to someone: "I know the name, but I can't replace the face."
9. While dining in a restaurant: "That waitress is all right, but she's unchattable."
10. When the Braves were in a slump: "We're just tiresome, that's all."
11. Discussing the Braves after being traded to Pittsburgh: "They're all right, but they've got too many young youths."
12. On the Braves' rebuilding program: "Rome wasn't born in a day."
13. Ordering dessert: "I'll have pie a la mode with ice cream."

Adds Wolf: "The only man I ever knew who came close to Logan in the world of crazy verbal-isms was the late Shorty Young, equipment manager of the Braves in 1953. Here are some Young-isms.

1. When his car was almost hit by another from the rear: "You almost knocked me through the windowshield."
2. Ordering breakfast: "I'll have bacon and eggs, and make my bacon cristy."
3. Complaining at breakfast: "It looks like they cut this ham with a raisin blade."
4. Explaining to players the procedure for taking a cab from the hotel to the ballpark: "Pay for the cab and Duffy (traveling secretary Duffy Lewis) will reverse you. And make sure you get a dippyduplate."
5. When the skies darkened and a storm seemed imminent: "It looks like a toronto."

As a player, manager, or after-dinner speaker, Leo Durocher has never been at a loss for words. But at the time of this photo, the start of the 1947 World Series, he had to do his audibles from the stands. The suspended manager of the Brooklyn Dodgers is with his then-wife, Laraine Day, and Danny Kaye.

UPI

Keith Morris' 24 Most Humorous After-Dinner Speakers on Sports

As Special Events and Publicity Director for *Sports Illustrated* as well as Director of *SI*'s Athletes Service Program and Speakers Bureau for more than 20 years, Keith Morris has led hundreds of sports celebrities to their roosting places on the rubber chicken circuit. They are in no particular order.

1. Joe Garagiola, baseball, TV
2. Tom Gorman, former major league umpire
3. Bob Uecker, baseball, TV
4. Ron Luciano, former major league umpire, TV analyst
5. Lou Holtz, football coach, Arkansas
6. Pete Carlesimo, former athletic director, Fordham
7. Bill Veeck, owner, Chicago White Sox
8. Jocko Conlan, former major league umpire
9. Hot Rod Hundley, former pro basketball star
10. Lee Trevino, golfer
11. Lefty Gomez, baseball Hall of Fame pitcher
12. Duffy Daugherty, former football coach, Michigan State
13. George Plimpton, author
14. Abe Lemons, basketball coach, University of Texas
15. Waite Hoyt, baseball Hall of Fame pitcher
16. Ned Harkness, hockey coach
17. Jim Bouton, former major league pitcher, author, columnist
18. Leo Durocher, former major league manager
19. Don Meredith, pro football, TV
20. Yogi Berra, baseball Hall of Fame catcher
21. Dick Vitale, former coach, Detroit Pistons
22. Jim Crowley, former Notre Dame football star
23. Satchel Paige, baseball Hall of Fame pitcher
24. Ben Martin, former football coach, Air Force Academy

XVIII

Water, Water, Everywhere

Frank Keating's 10 Favorite Fishing Holes

For more than 30 years, Frank Keating was an institution on Long Island as, first, the fishing editor of the Long Island *Daily Press* and, after its demise, the angler's angler for *Newsday*. As his list indicates, his fishing grounds were everywhere, from Lake Ontario to the Florida Keys, where he now lives in retirement of sorts. He's still fishing and he's still writing.

1. Bimini in May when the north-bound giant tuna surge through the Gulf Stream school after school.
2. Long Island's Montauk Point during October's full moon where the rips come alive with striped bass in the silvery light.
3. The coral reefs off Fort Jefferson in Florida's Dry Tortugas, home of the East Coast's huskiest groupers and slab-sided mutton snappers.

A while back, fishing columnist Frank Keating took his wife Helen on a canoe trip on the French River in Ontario. They caught muskies, pike, and bass.

Sports Photo Source

4. The Barrel Hole at Maine's Fourth Lake Musquacook (reached via Presque Isle) with its large and accommodating brook trout.
5. Looe Key on the Florida Keys outer reefs, a mecca for scuba divers and a grab-bag for anglers.
6. New York's Salmon River on Lake Ontario where the spring steelhead fishing is matched only by the fall runs of chinook and coho salmon.
7. Stellwagen Bank, off Gloucester, Mass., the late summer rallying ground for the fattest of giant bluefin tuna.
8. Cape May, New Jersey, with its vaunted schools of tiderunner weakfish, spring through fall.
9. New York's Walkill River, known among anglers aspiring only for size, as the "40-Mile Carp Stream."
10. The narrow, fast-flowing Hudson River at North Creek, N.Y., where energetic smallmouth bass hide behind every rock, to arouse every shore-caster.

10 Historic Surfing Leaders

1. King Kamehameha Nui—United the Hawaiian Islands into one kingdom in 1811, made the sport of surfing the national sport celebrated annually in a great Makahiki Festival, the Olympic Games of the Pacific.
2. Duke Paoa Kahanamoku—Born of royal blood in 1890, led Hawaii into the world's spotlight with his great victories in swimming in the 1912 Olympic Games and introduced surfing to many nations around the world.
3. George Douglas Freeth—Son of an Hawaiian princess and an American father, he was brought to the mainland by Henry Huntington from Hawaii in 1907; introduced surfing to the mainland at Redondo Beach; billed as "the man who walks on water."
4. Robert Simmons—Student at California Institute of Technology, his left arm crippled by a childhood accident, devoted to surfing but unable to carry the heavy wooden Hawaiian surfboards, created in 1953 the polyurethane surfboard used today which revolutionized the sport and popularized it around the world.

5. Dr. Hugh Bradner—While a student at the University of California, Berkeley, in 1951, invented the contemporary wet suit which made surfing a year-round sport even in cold waters by rejecting the long-held principle of trying to create a rubber suit to keep all water out. Bradner let a little in which, once warmed by body heat, also served to insulate the surfer from cold waters.
6. Thomas Edward Clark—All-American AAU swimmer, friend of Duke Kahanamoku, he created the first skeg (or fin) attached to the bottom of the surfboard to provide the surfer with greater control in steering the board; also invented the paddleboard used by lifeguards around the world today and for paddleboard events in surf competition.
7. Dr. Gary Fairmont R. Filosa II—Founder and first president in 1976 of the American Surfing Assn. (ASA) which brought surfing from chaos on the beaches into the AAU; founder and first president in 1976 of ICAS, the world surfing federation, which united 56 surfing countries to gain admission to the GAISF World Games in 1981 and to the Olympic Games in 1984 as a demonstration sport; the "Father of Olympic surfing."
8. Hobart Laidlaw Alter—Father of the fin box, a small box inserted to the bottom of the surfboard where a fin or skeg can be attached and replaced when needed by varying fins to meet varying wave conditions; also inventor of the Hobie Cat, a fast sailing catamaran.
9. Mary Lou Drummy—In a sport where women were second-class citizens, Mrs. Drummy led the fight and created the structure to give female surfers equal access to and equal recognition in the sport of surfing.
10. David G. Rivines—Former president of the AAU, he revived the ancient Hawaiian sport of paipo-surfing—surfing while prone on a bellyboard—in the lakes of Montana, the Dakotas, and Wyoming, creating the Junior Olympic Paipo Surfing program of the ASA.

SOURCE: The American Surfing Association.

The Top 10 American Men and Top 10 American Women Surfers

MEN

1. Mark Wildman
2. Bolton Colburn
3. Henry Noppenberger
4. Brian Howell
5. James Ingham
6. Bruce Reynolds Royer
7. George Haws
8. Winston Irebaria
9. Jeffrey Johnston
10. Douglas Brown

WOMEN

1. Dana Dawes
2. Susan Collins Pinnel
3. Gina Aubrey
4. Malana Sullivan
5. Joyce Fujioka
6. Cindy Morgan
7. Julie Dodd
8. Sharlene Diamond
9. Sandra Kurihara
10. Julienne Johnson

SOURCE: The American Surfing Association.

The Top 10 Surfers of All Time

1. King Kamahameha Nui
2. Duke Paoa Kahanamoku
3. James Jones
4. Peter Peterson
5. Thomas Edward Clark
6. Mark Richards
7. George Douglas Freeth
8. Eddie Aikau
9. Moroni Medeiros
10. Laura Bleers Ching

SOURCE: The American Surfing Association.

10 Celebrity Surfers

1. Duke Paoa Kahanamoku
2. King Kamehameha Nui
3. Dr. Gary Fairmont R. Filosa II
4. Richard Zanuck
5. Jack London
6. Otis Chandler
7. Senator Ted Stevens
8. The Prince of Wales
9. Hon. Charles Clark
10. Barry Goldwater, Jr.

SOURCE: The American Surfing Association.

XIX

Out Of The Crowd

The Boston *Globe*'s Ratings of the Most Unruly, Most Critical, and Most Knowledgeable Sports Fans

The Boston *Globe* took a poll of 97 sportswriters across the country to arrive at its results. The ratings follow, with first place votes in parentheses.

MOST UNRULY FANS

	POINTS
1. New York (45)	203
2. Philadelphia (4)	164
3. Boston-New England (11)	138
4. Chicago (5)	120
5. San Antonio (10)	76

MOST CRITICAL FANS

1. New York (20)	261
2. Philadelphia (36)	256
3. Boston-New England (15)	204
4. Chicago (2)	87
5. Los Angeles (3)	57

MOST KNOWLEDGEABLE FANS

1. New York (28)	236
2. Philadelphia (9)	198
3. Boston-New England (12)	95
4. Montreal (11)	88
5. Chicago (2)	70

RESULTS BY SPORT
FOOTBALL

MOST UNRULY

1. New York (10)	78
2. New England (10)	71
3. Philadelphia (1)	47
4. Cleveland (1)	23
5. Minnesota (1)	18

MOST CRITICAL

1. Philadelphia (9)	81
2. New York (6)	63
3. Los Angeles (3)	57
4. New England (4)	50
5. Chicago (1)	29

MOST KNOWLEDGEABLE

1. New York (7)	57
2. Philadelphia (4)	56
3. Pittsburgh (3)	44
4. Chicago (1)	31
5. Dallas (2)	29

BASKETBALL

MOST UNRULY

1. San Antonio (10)	76
2. Philadelphia (2)	39
3. Phoenix (5)	32
4. New York (1)	24
5. Boston	20

MOST CRITICAL

1. Philadelphia (9)	74
2. New York (6)	63
3. Boston (1)	30
4. Chicago	23
5. San Antonio (2)	16

MOST KNOWLEDGEABLE

1. New York (15)	96
2. Boston (3)	71
3. Philadelphia (2)	68
4. Portland	23
5. Milwaukee (1)	15

HOCKEY

MOST UNRULY

1. New York Rangers (15)	84
2. Chicago (3)	43
3. Philadelphia	37
4. Boston	28
5. New York Islanders	19

MOST CRITICAL

1. New York Rangers (7)	58
2. Montreal (5)	53
3. Boston (3)	46
4. Toronto	32
5. Quebec (3)	26

MOST KNOWLEDGEABLE

1. Montreal (11)	88
2. Toronto (6)	60
3. Boston (1)	47
4. Philadelphia	28
5. Buffalo (1)	19

BASEBALL

MOST UNRULY

1. New York (19)	117
2. Chicago (2)	77
3. Philadelphia (1)	41
4. Detroit (2)	37
5. San Francisco (1)	21

MOST CRITICAL

1. Philadelphia (18)	101
2. Boston (7)	78
3. New York (1)	77
4. Chicago (1)	35
5. Detroit and San Francisco	13

MOST KNOWLEDGEABLE

1. Boston (12)	95
2. New York (6)	83
3. Philadelphia (3)	46
4. Chicago (1)	39
5. Detroit (2)	36

Barry Janoff's 15 People Who Were in the Right Place, But in the Wrong Sport

1. Gene Tenace (baseball)
2. Jim Hunter (baseball)
3. George Archer (golf)
4. Trevor Hockey (soccer)
5. Matt Boxer (soccer)
6. Harvey Catchings (basketball)
7. Clint Hurdle (baseball)
8. Chet Walker (basketball)
9. Preacher Roe (baseball)
10. Mick Poole (soccer)
11. Terry Puhl (baseball)

Lou Miller, who operates without a stetho-
scope, checks Bob Turley's breathing.
Bill Greene/Sports Photo Source

12. Steve Trout (baseball)
13. and 14. Bobby Orr/Bobby Hull (hockey)
15. Wendy Turnbull (tennis)—Her last name is something a matador might yell in time of need.

Lou Miller's "11 Horses and Humans I Taught To Breathe"

Lou Miller competed and coached even while writing sports for the New York *World Telegram & Sun* from 1933 until its demise in 1966. After the Yankees' Bob Turley won two games and saved another in four World Series appearances in 1958, he revealed Miller had taught him to breathe properly, enabling him to become baseball's leading pitcher for the year.

Miller, promotions and communications staffman with the New York City Off-Track Betting Corp., also helped harness race horses and humans in a variety of other sports to relax, increase stamina and develop winning ways through special exercises that enlarged capacity for oxygen utilization.

1. Bob Turley—New York Yankee pitcher named baseball's Cy Young Award winner in 1958.
2. Joe Morrison—New York Football Giants' Mr. Everything who remained one of the NFL's most superbly conditioned performers, though one of its oldest, through his 14th and final Giant season in 1972.
3. Jim Beatty—North Carolina star who ran the first four-minute Madison Square Garden mile with a 3:59 in 1963.
4. Tom Courtney—Fordham U. flash who set a world 800-meter record in the 1956 Olympics in Melbourne.
5. George Glamack—An almost blind basketball center who sparked the Lou Miller-coached Office of Strategic Services (OSS) quintet to a Washington, D.C., area championship between the players' World War II missions. Glamack became a pro though he could hardly see the basket and hooked distance shots with his back to the basket.

6. John Quigley—DeLaSalle (N.Y.) schoolboy sprinter who upset Olympic champion Archie Williams in the Princeton Invitation quarter-mile in 1939.
7. Kenny Dares—A pacing horse Lou claimed for $10,000 who became a big-time winner in New York over pacers priced at $100,000.
8. Big Bill—One of the world's longest-lived horses, who celebrated his 40th birthday on January 1, 1981, at the Roosevelt-OTB Driving School. Forty years for a horse is the equivalent of 120 for a human.
9. Chief Gorge—A pacing horse Miller drove before deciding to confine himself almost exclusively to training and letting driving specialists do the steering.
10. Glen Direct N.—A New Zealand pacer who rose from lower rank to the highest in 1966 at the major New York tracks.
11. Bernard C.—A trotter who proved Miller's breath-taking interval sprint exercises could improve diagonal-gaited standardbreds as well as the pacers.

Furman Bisher's 10 Favorite Sports Names

Furman Bisher is the veteran and multi-talented sports editor and columnist for the Atlanta *Journal.*

1. Elmer Klumpp, baseball
2. Xavier Downwind, pro football
3. Ebenezer Goodfellow, hockey
4. Clarence Nottingham Churn, baseball
5. Emil Mashie, golf
6. Sterling Stryker, baseball
7. Bart Crashley, hockey
8. Colonel Lester (Bosco) Snover, baseball
9. Verl Lillywhite, football
10. Max Flack, baseball

Barry Janoff's 31 Sports Figures Born in October

Barry Janoff is a free-lance writer with an eye for the unusual.

October 1—Rod Carew, 1945
October 2—Maury Wills, 1932
October 3—Jean Ratelle, 1940
October 4—Sam Huff, 1934
October 5—Barry Switzer, 1937
October 6—Gary Gentry, 1946
October 7—Willie Naulls, 1934
October 8—Danny Murtaugh, 1917
October 9—Shep Messing, 1949
October 10—Peter Mahvolich, 1946
October 11—Rodney Marsh, 1944
October 12—Joe Cronin, 1906
October 13—Eddie Mathews, 1931
October 14—Lance Rentzel, 1943
October 15—Jim Palmer, 1945
October 16—Dave DeBusschere, 1940
October 17—Jim Gilliam, 1928
October 18—Willie Horton, 1942
October 19—Lonnie Shelton, 1955
October 20—Mickey Mantle, 1931
October 21—Whitey Ford, 1928
October 22—Jimmie Foxx, 1907
October 23—Pelé, 1940
October 24—Y.A. Tittle, 1926
October 25—Dave Cowens, 1948
October 26—Chuck Foreman, 1950
October 27—Ralph Kiner, 1922
October 28—Bruce Jenner, 1949
October 29—Dennis Potvin, 1953
October 30—Phil Chenier, 1950
October 31—John Lucas, 1953

Soccer devotees born on October 23 can enjoy something in common with the incomparable Pele.

Rich Pilling

Master batsman Rod Carew doesn't need tips from the astrologers.

Nancy Hogue

If George Washington were alive, he'd be celebrating Julius Erving's birthday.

Mitchell B. Reibel

10 Athletes Born on George Washington's Birthday

1. Julius Erving, 1950
2. Sparky Anderson, 1934
3. Connie Mack, 1862
4. and 5. Tom and Dick Van Arsdale, 1943
6. Ryne Duren, 1929
7. Steve Barber, 1939
8. Chet Walker, 1940
9. Dennis Awtrey, 1948
10. Tim Young, 1955

Barry Janoff's 13 Sports Figures with Namesakes in Another Field

1. George Burns: golf/actor
2. Jimmy Stewart: baseball/actor
3. Kit Carson: baseball/western hero
4. Danny Thomas: baseball/actor
5. Bob Hope: soccer/actor
6. George Kirby: soccer/comedian
7. Neil(l) Armstrong: football/astronaut
8. John Kennedy: baseball/politics
9. Tip O'Neill: baseball/politics
10. Jack Warner: baseball/movies
11. Eddie Fisher: baseball/singer
12. Cesar Romero: soccer/actor
13. Robert Shaw: baseball/actor

Pat McDonough's 7 Greatest Women Bowlers

Pat McDonough, publisher-editor-writer of the bowling paper, *Sports Reporter,* since 1967, has authored dozens of books and magazine articles on bowling. He covered sports, with an emphasis on bowling, for the New York *World-Telegram & Sun* from 1929 until its demise in 1966.

1. Marion Ladewig
2. Betty Morris
3. Patty Costello
4. Dotty Fothergill

5. Millie Martorella
6. Floretta McCutcheon
7. Marie Warmbier

Notes McDonough: "Few individuals have dominated a sport as did Marion Ladewig in women's bowling over a 15-year period, beginning in 1949. No less than eight times in that period she beat the top women in the All-Star Tournament.

"One can divide women's pro-bowling into three periods—pre-Ladewig, Ladewig and post-Ladewig. In the early period, Mrs. Floretta McCutcheon (No. 6) and Marie Warmbier (No. 7) dominated. In recent years, Betty Morris (No. 2) has been a standout. She won acclaim as Woman Bowler of the '70s in a poll of writers. Also ranking in the top echelon in the period starting in 1960 have been Millie Martorella (No. 5), Dotty Fothergill (No. 4) and Patty Costello (No. 3). Coincidentally, all are left-handers and all hail from the Northeast."

Jim Hawkins "8 Lists I'd Like To See, But Probably Never Will"

Jim Hawkins is sports columnist for the Detroit *Free Press*.

1. Jimmy Carter's favorite summer Olympics.
2. Howard Cosell's favorite vocabulary words.
3. Billy Martin's favorite general managers.
4. Steve Carlton's favorite sports writers.
5. Bob McAdoo's favorite defenses.
6. Charley Finley's favorite commissioners.
7. Jimmy Connors' favorite gestures.
8. Bud Grant's favorite Super Bowls.

No matter what, Jimmy Connors always has something for the crowd.

Wide World